T0339686

Cambridge Elements ≡

Elements in Ethics
edited by
Ben Eggleston
University of Kansas
Dale E. Miller
Old Dominion University, Virginia

ETHICAL REALISM

William J. FitzPatrick
University of Rochester

CAMBRIDGE
UNIVERSITY PRESS

CAMBRIDGE
UNIVERSITY PRESS

University Printing House, Cambridge CB2 8BS, United Kingdom

One Liberty Plaza, 20th Floor, New York, NY 10006, USA

477 Williamstown Road, Port Melbourne, VIC 3207, Australia

314–321, 3rd Floor, Plot 3, Splendor Forum, Jasola District Centre,
New Delhi – 110025, India

103 Penang Road, #05–06/07, Visioncrest Commercial, Singapore 238467

Cambridge University Press is part of the University of Cambridge.

It furthers the University's mission by disseminating knowledge in the pursuit of
education, learning, and research at the highest international levels of excellence.

www.cambridge.org
Information on this title: www.cambridge.org/9781108706414
DOI: 10.1017/9781108580885

First published 2022

A catalogue record for this publication is available from the British Library.

ISBN 978-1-108-70641-4 Paperback
ISSN 2516-4031 (online)
ISSN 2516-4023 (print)

Ethical Realism

Elements in Ethics

DOI: 10.1017/9781108580885
First published online: January 2022

William J. FitzPatrick
University of Rochester

Author for correspondence: William J. FitzPatrick, william.fitzpatrick@rochester.edu

Abstract: This Element examines the many facets of ethical realism and the issues at stake in metaethical debates about it – both between realism and non-realist alternatives, and between different versions of realism itself. Starting with a minimal core characterization of ethical realism focused on claims about meaning and truth, we go on to develop a narrower and more theoretically useful conception by adding further claims about objectivity and ontological commitment. Yet even this common understanding of ethical realism captures a surprisingly heterogeneous range of views. In fact, a strong case can be made for adding several more conditions in order to arrive at a paradigm of realism about ethics when understood in a non-deflationary way. We then develop this more robust realism, bringing out its distinctive take on ethical objectivity and normative authority, its unique ontological commitments, and both the support for it and some challenges it faces.

Keywords: metaethics, ethical realism, normativity, nonnaturalism, objective value

ISBNs: 9781108706414 (PB), 9781108580885 (OC)
ISSNs: 2516-4031 (online), 2516-4023 (print)

Contents

Introduction

Metaethics takes up questions about the semantics, metaphysics, and epistemology of the ethical domain. Stepping back from engaged ethical practice itself, we ask higher-order questions about the sort of meaning ethical terms and statements have, about the existence and nature of ethical properties and facts, and about whether and how we can have knowledge of them. Ethical realism is the metaethical view that the ethical domain is to be understood on a *realist* model, providing realist answers to such questions. But what exactly counts as a "realist" construal of the ethical domain? What exactly must one be realist about and what does that involve? And why does it matter?

How we answer these questions will turn partly on what we think makes for the most illuminating classificatory scheme in metaethics, given our primary theoretical concerns. This leads to some variation in taxonomic choices, reflecting different priorities. Certain starting assumptions may make a difference too. Some might assume, for example, that realism in the ethical domain should closely mirror realism in other domains, such as mathematics or the sciences, with analogous commitments regarding meaning, truth, and objectivity. Such an approach might be misleading, however, if it turns out (as I will argue) that there are elements unique to ethics that require additional theoretical treatment by any non-deflationary realism *about ethics*. Ethical realism may therefore have a distinctive profile, building in more than other forms of realism do.

We'll begin, in Section 1, by laying out the broadest conception of ethical realism – what I'll call the "minimal core characterization" involving two fundamental claims – and then proceed to examine the reasons for adding two additional claims to arrive at a narrower characterization that is both more useful in dividing the conceptual space of metaethics and arguably more deserving of the realist label. This more filled-out characterization reflects the most common understanding of ethical realism in contemporary metaethics, given various complications introduced in recent decades. I will go on to argue in Section 2, however, that even this more refined conception remains too broad: for it is possible to meet those first four conditions while still failing to capture certain apparent elements of ethics in a way that a *realism about ethics* plausibly should. This position will be controversial, but I believe a strong case can be made for it.

In Section 2 we will go on to explore what seems to be missing so far and add further conditions to our characterization, arriving at a more adequate paradigm of ethical realism, as developed in Section 3. Given, however, that it would be revisionary to restrict our use of "ethical realism" to views that build in so much, we will continue to count the broader class of views satisfying the first four conditions as forms of ethical realism, and refer to the more robust version as "ardent ethical realism."[1] We will conclude, in Section 4, with an examination of support for and challenges faced by ethical realism, especially in its more robust form.

While this Element is designed to be accessible to a broad readership, without presupposing prior knowledge of metaethics, it goes into some depth on issues that will be of interest to readers already familiar with the field as well. Readers new to metaethics can safely ignore many of the footnotes and are encouraged to consult other Elements in this series for detailed treatments of rival metaethical views that can only be sketched here in the course of situating and elucidating ethical realism.

1 What Is Ethical Realism?

1.1 The Minimal Core Characterization of Ethical Realism

Consider a typical ethical belief you might hold, such as the belief that human trafficking is morally wrong. On the face of it, such beliefs are likely to strike you both as *meaningful* and as capable of being *true* in the same sense in which ordinary descriptive beliefs can be true. In this respect, ethical beliefs or claims appear to function very much like other beliefs or claims. Ethical realism begins with this plausible idea that we use ethical language to make claims that can be straightforwardly true or false, just as with claims in other spheres of discourse, and that at least some positive ethical claims are in fact true. On this approach, then, there are some ethical truths alongside truths in the sciences and mathematics, for example. We can express these ideas more precisely with the following two claims:

> (1) **Representational Content**: Ethical sentences, such as "human trafficking is morally wrong," express propositions that can be straightforwardly true or false, just as with ordinary descriptive sentences. More specifically, when construed literally they are true or false by virtue of their *representational ethical content* – that is, content that represents an ethical fact or state of affairs as obtaining, as by representing human trafficking as having the property of being morally wrong. Ethical sentences and propositions, just like descriptive ones, are *truth-apt* due to their representational content, and ethical claims purport to state ethical facts. Likewise, our ethical judgments are *cognitive* states – beliefs – with the same representational ethical content. Ethical claims express such beliefs, which can likewise be straightforwardly true or false, just as with other beliefs.

---

[1] I borrow the expression "ardent realism" from Matti Eklund (2017), with qualifications discussed later. Eklund does not himself endorse the view.

(2) **Truth**: At least some positive ethical sentences, and the propositions expressed by them, are in fact *true*, and straightforwardly so, in the way ordinary descriptive sentences or propositions are: they are true because the world is in fact as it is represented to be by the propositional content in question. The difference between ethical and ordinary descriptive sentences or propositions is that what is represented by the content of the former is an *evaluative* or *normative* state of affairs (e.g., that human trafficking is morally wrong) and not simply a descriptive state of affairs (e.g., that human trafficking causes suffering). Since some positive ethical claims are true, there are likewise *ethical properties and facts*. It is in virtue of such properties and facts that some of our positive ethical claims succeed in being *true*, that is, when they accurately represent a state of affairs involving the instantiation of ethical properties.

These two theoretical commitments constitute what we may call the "minimal core characterization" of ethical realism, and they already set realism apart from several competing metaethical views.

The first commitment, when properly understood, excludes traditional *non-cognitivism* and its more recent outgrowth, non-realist (or anti-realist or quasi-realist) *expressivism*. According to such views, ethical language and concepts have a fundamentally different function from ordinary descriptive language and concepts. Instead of being used to represent ethical facts or states of affairs – such as the fact that human trafficking is wrong – they are primarily used *to express certain attitudes or commitments or plans* – such as an attitude of disapproval toward human trafficking or a commitment to avoid it – *without* thereby purporting to represent any ethical state of affairs as obtaining (Gibbard 1990, 2003, 2006; Horgan and Timmons 2000, 2008). The first realist claim rejects this construal of how ethical language and concepts work, insisting that ethical judgments have representational content just as other familiar judgments do (even if they can obviously *also* be used to express attitudes or commitments).[2]

---

[2] This point is complicated by the fact that sophisticated non-realist expressivists have adopted minimalist construals of "truth," "proposition," "property," "belief," and perhaps even "representation" that *derivatively* enable them to *say*, in the end, most of the same things realists say about these things, muddying the difference between the positions (Dreier 2004). For example, on a minimalist conception of truth, to say that it is *true* that murder is wrong (or that "murder is wrong" is *true*) is nothing more than to say that murder is wrong. So anyone who judges that murder is wrong is entitled to say that it is *true* that murder is wrong – even on an expressivist account of moral judgment, where it is simply a matter of having or expressing a certain attitude or commitment. And if murder's having the *property* of being wrong is understood to mean no more than that wrongness is truly predicated of murder, then again judging that murder is wrong (even under an expressivist construal) entitles us to speak of murder's "having the property" of being wrong. So the expressivist can say, in a sense, that there are moral properties and moral truths. There can similarly be minimalist talk of "believing" murder to be wrong insofar as one takes it to be wrong, and even of thereby "representing" murder as having the property of being wrong. The difference, however, is that while the expressivist may be able to say these realist-sounding things in a minimalist sense at the end of the day, their *route* to this is very

The second realist claim, about the existence of ethical truths, excludes *error theory* or *metaethical nihilism*. According to such views, all positive ethical claims – such as the claim that human trafficking is wrong – are false. Unlike the expressivist views mentioned previously, error-theoretic views agree with the realist's first claim about the representational function of ethical language and concepts. The problem, they maintain, is that positive ethical claims are defective insofar as they presuppose the existence of certain properties that (according to error theorists) do not in fact exist, such as objective values, thus making all such claims false (Mackie 1977).[3] The realist's second claim rejects this error-theoretic assessment, claiming instead that at least many positive ethical claims are straightforwardly true rather than saddled with error. This claim also likely excludes crude forms of subjectivism or relativism involving such distorted interpretations of ethical claims that they flout platitudes associated with the meaning of ethical concepts, thus failing to make any ethical claims come out as true when construed *literally* (Sayre-McCord 1988).

Now those who are primarily concerned with the issues in claims one and two, and so with excluding expressivism, error theory, and crude forms of subjectivism or relativism, might be happy to stop with this minimal core characterization of ethical realism. Notice, however, that nothing has yet been said about the *source* of ethical truth. In particular, there is so far no requirement that it be *objective* rather than subjective (as long as the account respects platitudes constitutive of the meanings of ethical concepts). On the minimal core characterization, ethical realism is ecumenical on this front.[4] This approach therefore still leaves us with an extremely heterogeneous collection of metaethical views under the umbrella of ethical realism – including many that are commonly placed into distinct metaethical categories typically viewed as *rivals* to realism, such as various forms of ethical constructivism.[5]

---

different from the realist's. The nonrealist expressivist says these things in a minimalist sense after providing an account of the semantics of moral discourse radically different from that of ordinary descriptive discourse, whereas the realist takes the chief semantic role of moral language to be the same as with ordinary descriptive language, such that moral language is used in the first instance to make assertions about the instantiation of properties that are as metaphysically robust as any others (Copp 2007, ch. 5). Or as Dreier (2004) emphasizes, whereas nonrealist expressivists do not *need* to make any appeal to any notion of moral properties in explaining what it is to make a moral judgment, realists must do so.

[3] Although Mackie (1977) is standardly understood to be the paradigm error theorist, Selim Berker (2019) argues that Mackie himself did not in fact espouse error theory as formulated earlier.

[4] Sayre-McCord (1988, 16) holds that "realism is not solely the prerogative of objectivists," and takes any independence of ethical truth to be relevant only insofar as it might bear on the second claim (since accounts proposing certain kinds of dependence on us would fail to secure the truth of ethical claims construed literally).

[5] See, for example, Sharon Street (2006, 2008b), who explicitly presents her subjectivist metaethical constructivism as an *anti*-realist view that avoids the Darwinian Dilemma she raises against realist views.

For example, *subjectivist constructivist* views allow for positive ethical truths but take them to be grounded in facts about hypothetical attitudes, desires, or other responses we would have if we applied some sort of idealizing procedure to our existing psychology; ethical truths are constructed from or derived *via* some such procedure applied to our mental states or activities. The procedure in question is meant to be specifiable in an ethically neutral way – for example, involving procedural deliberative exercises starting from our existing attitudes with improved empirical information – so that ethical truth can be fully explained without circularity, appealing only to psychological and procedural facts.[6] Similarly, ideal observer or appraiser views seek to derive ethical truths from the responses or judgments of a hypothetical agent occupying some ideal perspective (again characterized without ethical assumptions). And neo-Kantian constructivist or *constitutivist* views take ethical truths to be a function of principles bound up with procedures constitutive of the exercise of rational agency as such. On this approach, ethical truths are *constructed* through such practically necessary procedures rather than being already *there to be discovered* in the world in the way that biological or physical truths are (Korsgaard 1996, 2009).

These views seem to satisfy the minimal core characterization of ethical realism: they are compatible with the representationalist semantics and cognitivism given in the first claim and they allow for the existence of positive ethical truths as posited by the second claim.[7] But again, they are also generally viewed today as alternatives to ethical realism rather than as paradigms of it, and for good reason. If we construe ethical realism as broadly as the minimal core characterization proposes then we wind up capturing everything from subjectivist constructivism (with ethical facts constrained by our desires or attitudes) or neo-Kantian constitutivism (with ethical facts arising only through procedures associated with our exercise of agency) to a robust platonic objectivism (with ethical facts rooted in transcendent, timeless values). So unless our principal theoretical concerns in metaethics are just with the issues laid out in the minimal core characterization, it is doubtful that such a heterogeneous collection of views makes for a particularly useful metaethical category.

For many of us at least, issues concerning the source of ethical truth or the nature of ethical facts are no less central to our metaethical concerns than the semantic issues emphasized in the minimal core characterization. This is reflected in the association of ethical realism with views that used to be called

---

[6] See Williams (1981) for the classic employment of this strategy in accounting for normative reasons.

[7] The situation with neo-Kantian constructivism is actually a bit tricky: it may wind up violating the second claim, as discussed below.

"ethical objectivism," embodying a commitment not only to the basic claims about meaning and truth but also to some notion of *objective ethical reality*. While it is complicated what exactly this means, as we'll see, the rough idea is that there exists a set of ethical properties and facts that are *there to be discovered or recognized* – not necessarily in the world *apart* from human beings and relevant facts about human life, but at least *there in the human-involving world* in a way that does not involve being constructed from elements or acts of human psychology in the ways described earlier.

The difference we're after is clearest in the case of neo-Kantian constructivism. On this view, while we may speak of ethical truth, it is *derivative*. We begin with certain procedures or deliberative rules that are allegedly necessary for exercising agency at all, and then we identify principles allegedly bound up with those procedures (such as Kant's categorical imperative), which then count as "correct" or "true" *not* because they track existing ethical facts but simply because they spring from those practically necessary procedures; such principles and their implications (e.g., that we have a duty not to lie) can then be regarded as "ethical truths or facts" in this derivative sense rooted in necessary agential procedures. By contrast, an ethical realism that incorporates objectivity begins by positing *non*derivative ethical facts that serve as the truth-makers for true ethical claims. If there are correct procedures for answering ethical questions, then those procedures will count as correct because they or the principles they yield *accurately track* those existing ethical facts (not because they play a practically necessary or constitutive role in exercising agency, for example).[8]

The situation is a little different with subjectivist constructivist views that instead apply idealizing procedures, such as deliberation with full empirical information, to desires or attitudes. Here the issue isn't that the notion of truth itself is taken to be derivative in ethics, as on the neo-Kantian approach mentioned earlier, but just that the various ethical truths have as their truth-makers a complex set of facts involving our subjective states and the results of

---

[8] Korsgaard (1996, 36) characterizes her neo-Kantian constructivism as "procedural realism," since it allows for ethical truths or facts, though only in this procedurally-based way; and she contrasts this with "substantive realism," which takes ethical facts to exist in a more straightforward (nonderivative, procedurally independent) way. Ethical realism is generally understood as substantive realism, which means that we need to add a further condition to the minimal core characterization to exclude merely procedural views. It might be argued, however, that the minimal core characterization already excludes neo-Kantian procedural realism: the second realist claim may eliminate such views already on the grounds that they fail to make some ethical claims *literally and straightforwardly true or false*, since they employ a nonstandard, derivative notion of truth. Indeed, Korsgaard's view makes the notion of ethical truth a theoretical *afterthought*, given the view's radically practical orientation in reducing normativity to a form of practical necessity for exercising agency (FitzPatrick 2005). In any case, our characterization of ethical realism needs to exclude such approaches, either with the second claim or through the independence condition added later.

hypothetical procedural exercises. This isn't offering a revised notion of *what it is* for certain principles or claims to count as *true*, but just a subjectively oriented claim about what *grounds* ethical truths or facts, based on what ethical claims are allegedly really about – namely, some idealized function of our mental states. Still, this kind of dependence of ethical truths or facts on contingent facts about our desires and attitudes stands in stark contrast with views that posit ethical facts that are not dependent on our psychologies in that way.

For all these reasons, it is theoretically useful to build more into our characterization of ethical realism than we get from minimal core characterization, adding constraints on the source or grounds of ethical truth to capture some idea of *objective ethical reality*. We'll take this up in the following subsection, though I'll argue in Section 2 that even this is insufficient to capture the objectivity that ultimately matters to non-deflationary realism about ethics. But this is still an important step along the way.

1.2 Adding Objectivity/Independence

I have proposed adding to our characterization of ethical realism an objectivity or independence condition to capture the idea that the source or grounds of ethical truth are in some interesting way *independent of us*. How exactly to characterize this condition, however, is complicated.

Ethical truths are, after all, largely *about* us (how it is good and right for us to live and to treat each other) and on any plausible view their grounds will often involve facts about us. Part of what *makes* human trafficking wrong (and hence makes true the claim that it is wrong) is the fact that it causes suffering in its victims – a fact obviously not independent of human beings. Similarly, the truth of ethical claims about moral blameworthiness or desert will depend partly on facts about agents' epistemic states (knowledge or ignorance of relevant circumstances) and intentions and motives – again, all facts about human beings and so hardly "independent of us." Many particular ethical truths will even depend on social conventions. If someone does something wrong in making a gesture because this amounts to a gratuitous insult, then part of what makes the giving of that gesture wrong will be facts about its conventional meaning in the social context.

The independence we're seeking, therefore, requires careful unpacking. As a first pass, we might characterize it by saying that despite the aforementioned forms of dependence, there is a true or correct set of *ethical standards*, from which particular ethical truths are derived, and these standards will not themselves depend on such things as our ethical beliefs or conventions, or on our contingent desires, attitudes, commitments, choices, and so on – either directly or indirectly *via* idealizing procedures of the sort described earlier. Russ Shafer-Landau helpfully formulates this as a *stance-independence* condition, which we may add to our initial two claims:

> (3) **Stance-Independence**: There are positive "[ethical] truths that obtain independently of any preferred perspective in the sense that *the [ethical] standards that fix the [particular ethical] facts are not made true or correct by virtue of their ratification from within any given actual or hypothetical perspective*," such as one employing idealizing conditions or procedures
> (Shafer-Landau 2003, 15).

With the addition of this condition, ethical realism takes on a commitment to a set of *objective ethical standards* in this stance-independence sense. We've said that a central wrong-making feature of human trafficking – a feature that makes it wrong and hence makes true the claim that it is wrong – is the fact that it causes human suffering. This latter, empirical fact about the effects of human trafficking – call it "CHS" – is obviously not something that is independent of humans. But the stance-independence condition is drawing attention to a different fact posited within this picture: namely, the *evaluative or normative meta*-fact *that* CHS is wrong-making (cf. Dancy 2006). Our third claim, about stance-independence, is concerned with such ethical meta-facts, because such meta-facts (suitably generalized and qualified) are what constitute the ethical standards referred to in our third claim.

To keep things simple, let's focus on ethical standards concerning *rightness* of action. An account of these standards will articulate a set of claims about which features of actions tend to be right-making and which tend to be wrong-making, how various circumstances might affect these tendencies (e.g., making for exceptions to typical wrong-makingness in certain circumstances), and how to weigh complex sets of factors to arrive at an overall assessment of an action as right or wrong based on all its features and circumstances. Such an account of the ethical standards thus tells us what acts must be like – the conditions they must meet with regard to their relevant features – in order to qualify as right and avoid coming out as wrong. On some views, the ethical standards might be given with a single ultimate rule or principle, while on others – such as a virtue-theoretic account – they may be far more complex and less codifiable, involving a plurality of considerations and a need for educated judgment to determine how exactly they interact to yield all-things-considered verdicts in complex cases.[9]

---

[9] We may here set aside debates over the degree to which the ethical standards are codifiable in terms of one or more principles, though I will tend to discuss them using a pluralistic, virtue-theoretic framework, which I favor.

A nonethical analogy may help to illustrate the idea of evaluative standards and their role in connection with evaluative properties (further developed in Section 2). Consider the standards for being a good move in chess. An account of this will articulate a set of claims about features of a chess move that tend to count as good-making (e.g., increasing control of the center squares) and features that instead tend to count as bad-making (e.g., sacrificing material without positional or tactical gain), along with the differences that various circumstances can make and how to weigh complex sets of factors to arrive at an overall assessment. The standards constituted by such propositions tell us what a chess move needs to be like in order to constitute a good move and avoid being a bad one (allowing room for gradations and qualifications). With such a set of standards in hand, we are then in a position to evaluate a given chess move as a good or bad one based on whether its overall features, in the circumstances, make it meet or violate those standards.

In the case of chess, the standards that fix the particular facts about good or bad chess moves are grounded in – or made true or correct by virtue of – the rules and aims internal to the game. Obviously, the model for ethics will be different, and our characterization of ethical realism has not yet provided one. What we are adding with the third claim, however, is at least a negative point about how *not* to understand the source of the ethical standards: they are not grounded in (or made true or correct by virtue of) being ratified from within some actual or hypothetical perspective, as on constructivist views. It tells us, for example, that whatever exactly it is that grounds the correct set of standards for ethically evaluating human action, it is not to be found in any such fact as that we would endorse these standards if we underwent certain deliberative exercises starting from our existing attitudes with full empirical information. According to the realist's third claim, whatever grounds ethical standards, it is not any sort of *stance-dependent under-writing*, as by deriving the standards from the application of ethically neutrally specifiable sets of conditions or procedures to our beliefs, desires, attitudes, agential capacities, conventions, and so on.[10]

Importantly, this is not to deny that ethical standards might still be grounded largely in facts about human beings or human life. It is consistent with the third

---

[10] We noted earlier that neo-Kantian constructivism might in a way be further from ethical realism than subjectivist constructivism, insofar as it employs a derivative notion of truth. There is also, however, a sense in which it may be *closer* to ethical realism in connection with the objectivity or independence issue: for although neo-Kantian constructivism violates the third condition we've now laid down, just as subjectivist constructivism does, the former at least avoids making certain core ethical facts (such as moral duties) dependent on the details of our contingent psychological states: we will (allegedly) wind up with the categorical imperative regardless of what contingent desires or attitudes we start out with, which thus secures *independence* from at least the contingent details of human psychology (Korsgaard 1996).

claim, for example, that there is a correct set of ethical standards consisting partly in requirements to respect human dignity, where human dignity is an evaluative or normative status grounded in facts about human rational capacity. To be consistent with the third claim, we simply have to hold that this fact about the evaluative or normative ramifications of human rational capacity is itself an objective evaluative or normative fact about it. All that is denied is that this fact itself is somehow dependent on being ratified from within some actual or hypothetical perspective. It is thus worth emphasizing again that the third claim does not commit ethical realism to any transcendental or radically independent grounding of the ethical standards wholly apart from facts about human life: it simply insists that the grounding of the ethical standards is a stance-independent matter in the sense described.[11]

1.3 Metaphysical Matters

Assuming that ethical realism posits some sort of objective or stance-independent ethical reality, we may now ask whether this brings with it *metaphysical* commitments. In particular, does ethical realism require us to add such things as ethical properties and facts to our ontology, as part of the fabric of (relevant parts of) the world or reality? It is natural to think that it does, and that when our ethical claims are true they are *made* to be true by accurately representing that ethical reality. For example, a realist might think that part of what grounds the ethical standard forbidding cruelty is the fact that the suffering of sentient beings is intrinsically bad – an evaluative fact about the world consisting in the possession of an evaluative property (badness) by a worldly phenomenon (suffering). In this picture, the ethical truth that causing suffering for amusement is wrong has this worldly evaluative fact as (at least part of) its *truth-maker*: the ethical claim is true because of how the world is, ethically speaking – specifically, because of a real evaluative property possessed by suffering.

Some metaethicists, such as Derek Parfit, however, embrace objective ethical truths but deny that they have any such ontological implications for the world or reality, or indeed that they have (or need) any truth-makers at all, any more than logical or mathematical truths do. More precisely, these theorists will allow that some nonbasic ethical truths might have "truth-makers" in the sense that they are derived from more basic ethical truths: for example, the truth of "causing

---

[11] Note that the ethical standards might still perfectly *correspond* to what would be ratified from some ideal perspective: the claim is just that this is not what would *make* the standards the true or correct ones (cf. Shafer-Landau 2003, 16). It would be the other way around: the perspective that wound up endorsing those standards would count as ideal because it accurately tracked the true or correct standards and their implications.

suffering for amusement is *wrong*" might be explicable in terms of a more basic but still normative truth such as "there is strong *reason* for anyone to avoid causing suffering for amusement" (see Parfit 2011 and Scanlon 2014 on "reasons fundamentalism"). But they claim that *basic* normative truths *would not themselves have any truth-makers anywhere in the world*: they would not be made to be true by any real properties of anything in the world or by the way any part of the world is. On this view, such propositions are simply true without being made true by "how things are in some part of reality," and so they have no ontological implications for the sorts of properties the world contains, any more than logical or mathematical truths do (Parfit 2017, 58 f.). As Parfit puts it: they "are not about metaphysical reality, since they do not imply that certain things exist in some ontological sense" (2011, 749).[12]

We can formulate this claim in terms of the ethical meta-facts and standards discussed earlier (and at greater length later). Let CSA be the empirical property an act can have of causing suffering for amusement, and let EMF be the ethical meta-fact that the fact that an act has property CSA is wrong-making. Parfit's claim is that *EMF has no truth-maker*: nothing makes it true; it just is true. EMF is also not "about metaphysical reality," representing how things are in a normative part of reality, any more than logical truths are about some part of metaphysical reality. The same goes for the true or correct set of ethical standards realists posit, of which truths such as EMF are constitutive: they are correct or true, but, as with logical truths, nothing, in reality, makes them so and they have no ontological implications since they are not about reality in any ontological sense.[13]

Now although this sort of view might be regarded as a "non-metaphysical" version of ethical realism, given its endorsement of our first three claims, it's noteworthy that Parfit himself rejected that classification in favor of "*Non-Realist* Cognitivism" – explicitly distancing his view from ethical realism (Parfit 2017). And this taxonomic move makes good sense in light of the natural association we have noted between ethical realism and the idea that ethical

---

[12] Parfit isn't denying that *specific* ethical truths involving worldly particulars are "about metaphysical reality" and are made true partly by "how things are in some part of reality." The ethical truth that *Smith is wronging Jones* is obviously about metaphysical reality and it will be made true partly by some such worldly fact as that Smith is gratuitously insulting Jones. The ethical truths that lack truth-makers, according to Parfit, are what Scanlon (2014, 36–37) calls "pure normative claims," which do not involve particulars in that way. For Parfit, nothing *in the world* makes it true that there is reason not to cause suffering for amusement and that so acting is wrong, just as nothing in the world makes it true that there are infinitely many prime numbers.

[13] For critical worries about such a view, see e.g., Suikkanen (2017), Copp (2018), FitzPatrick (2018a), and Mintz-Woo (2018). It is especially puzzling, I think, how there could be substantive ethical truths that are *not made true by anything* but nonetheless somehow still have an authoritative claim to our deepest attention and concern in governing our practical lives.

properties and facts are part of the fabric of *reality* or the *world*, serving as real truth-makers for true ethical claims. It is hard to reconcile an unqualified claim to *ethical realism* with the denial that reality has anything in the way of ethical value or normativity within its ontology or that ethical claims are grounded in or even about reality! Therefore, while allowing that for some purposes we might still wish to count such views as broadly realist, I propose adding a fourth condition to our characterization of ethical realism proper:

> (4) **Ontological Commitment**: Basic ethical truths, which are constitutive of the true or correct set of ethical standards that fix particular ethical facts, have truth-makers within the ontology of the world/reality (in the form of worldly ethical properties and facts).

This builds explicitly into our characterization of ethical realism an ontological commitment to objective ethical reality – ethical truths grounded in the very reality or world in which we live (or on more Platonic views, at least in some similarly ontologically weighty part of reality). The details of such grounding will of course vary across different realist views, and the claim is deliberately left vague so far to cover a range of views, including both naturalistic and nonnaturalistic versions of realism. The point is just that there should be some ontological commitment of the sort given in the fourth claim.[14]

That said, there is a complication that may require an exception to claim 4. Terence Cuneo and Russ Shafer-Landau (2014) have advanced a view that is similar to Parfit's in rejecting claim 4, though they maintain that their view is nonetheless ontologically committed and is a form of ethical realism. They hold that core substantive moral truths – which they call the "moral fixed points" – such as "it is wrong to impose agony on others solely for personal gain" – are nonnatural *conceptual* truths: moral propositions that are "true in virtue of the nature of the non-natural moral concepts that constitute them" (411, 403). Like Parfit, then, they deny that moral truths "require . . . worldly truth-makers," that is, corresponding nonnatural moral properties and facts in the world, to "render them true": on their view these core moral propositions are made true by their constituent *concepts*, and the view is neutral on whether there even *are* any corresponding properties and facts in the world at all (411, 403). So they reject claim 4. Yet they also reject Parfit's disavowal of ontological commitment and take their view to have real ontological commitments (400), thus counting as a form of nonnaturalistic ethical *realism*.[15]

---

[14] This taxonomic choice is further supported by Parfit's (2017, 64) own conclusion that his Non-Realist Cognitivism winds up more or less converging with cognitivist versions of *Anti-Realist or Quasi-Realist Expressivism*.

[15] The notion of "non-naturalism" is discussed in Section 3.2.

We need not here go into the details surrounding their case for a different, derivative sort of ontological commitment, which would take us too far afield for present purposes. The point to note here is just that there will be cases like this where the classificatory choice – whether to count a view as realist or not, on metaphysical grounds – is not obvious and we can be flexible about it, perhaps allowing some exceptions to claim 4 if a compelling case is made. Either way, what really matters is just to appreciate the various issues in play here.[16]

1.4 Are We There Yet?

We have articulated and unpacked four central claims so far in characterizing ethical realism:

(1) **Representational Content**: about the semantics of ethical discourse;
(2) **Truth**: about the existence of positive ethical truths;
(3) **Stance-Independence**: about the relevant independence or objectivity of those truths; and
(4) **Ontological Commitment**: about the ontological commitment implied by ethical truths.

It might seem that with these four central claims, we have now captured everything relevant to ethical realism as such. Any view satisfying these four conditions, one might think, must surely count as paradigmatically realist about ethics, and any further variations would merely be differences of detail among *equally realist* metaethical views. Indeed, this is very likely the standard view.

Nonetheless, I believe it is mistaken, for reasons brought out in the next section. There is a strong case to be made for thinking that we have not yet reached a paradigm of full-blooded ethical realism – one that is realist about ethics conceived in a non-deflationary way. This will, of course, be controversial, but it is worth exploring because it brings into focus what may matter distinctively about *ethics*, which needs to be captured by paradigmatic ethical realism. The reflections raised in the next section suggest that ethics has distinctive features that require more for genuine realism in this domain.

To foreshadow: we need to build more into our conception of what it takes for something to be an *ethical* truth, to properly capture the fundamental

---

[16] A significant challenge for such a concept-based view is that it remains unclear how conceptual truths, which are not made true by anything we might encounter in the world in which we live and act as ethical agents – for example, by normative properties or facts involving the badness of suffering or dignity of persons – could have the categorical normative authority ethical truths seem to have for us, as we will discuss in Section 3.

realist idea that "reality itself favors certain ways of valuing and acting" (as Matti Eklund 2017, has helpfully put it), where this favoring involves a categorical normative authority. This will require adding to the four conditions we've laid out so far. Since the convention has been to label views that accept those first four claims as "realist" ones, I will do the same to avoid confusion. But I believe a truly paradigmatic realism (to which I'll give the label "ardent ethical realism") needs to incorporate claims 5–8 in the next two sections as well.

2 Going Further: Why More Is Plausibly Needed

What exactly is it that we need to be realist *about* in the ethical domain in order to have a paradigmatic ethical realism? The answer may seem obvious: ethics, of course! But what does that mean? We have so far been cashing this out in terms of various claims about *ethical truths*, using a few examples to illustrate, but we haven't yet said much about what it takes for something to *be* an ethical truth in the first place. And the problem is that there are ways of thinking about what ethical properties and truths consist in that may readily yield objective and ontology-involving "ethical truths" but arguably still fail to deliver crucial elements of *ethics* – missing the very things we'd need to be realists about in order to be full-blooded ethical realists.

2.1 Missing the Target with Truths that Come Too Easily

On a realist view, ethical truths are truths involving ethical concepts (such as the concept of moral wrongness), which latter pick out ethical properties (such as the property of moral wrongness), which are constituents of ethical facts (such as the fact that human trafficking is morally wrong). So what, then, are ethical concepts (and corresponding ethical properties)? What does it take for a concept (or property) to be an *ethical* one? A common thought here – one amenable to the idea that ethical thought and practice are natural, evolved phenomena – is that ethical concepts are those that play certain practical roles in guiding human deliberation and action. More specifically, they do so *via* internalized social norms for coordinating behavior, reinforced by social approval or criticism, praise/reward, or blame/punishment. As part of our Darwinian heritage and subsequent cultural evolution, we have evolved a disposition to develop and employ such concepts and norms in regulating social life. *Ethical* concepts, then, are those that play this role in normative governance or guidance, as part of natural human social functioning (Gibbard 1990; Kitcher 2006, 2011).

This gives a sense to the notion of an ethical concept and norm that is also employed by cultural anthropologists, evolutionary psychologists, historians, and others studying human thought and behavior. To get ethical truths on the table, then, we just need for it to be the case that:

(i)   some of these concepts succeed in picking out *properties*,
(ii) claims employing these concepts function to *ascribe* those properties to things, thus purporting to state truths, and
(iii) some of them succeed in doing so, *accurately representing* the things in question as having those properties.

This would seem to give us ethical concepts, ethical properties, and ethical truths. And if the truth conditions for these ethical claims are objective and ontology-involving – for example, if the properties in question are objective natural properties – then we would seem to have satisfied all four conditions so far laid out for ethical realism.

While this may seem like good news for ethical realism, however, it actually raises a serious worry. We might wonder: Do such ethical truths perhaps come *too easily*, in a way that actually undermines the very things we wanted in realism about ethical value and normativity to begin with? To see the problem, imagine how easily this scenario might come about:

> Suppose a community develops linguistic practices and behavior-regulating norms involving a term "W" and concept of W-ness, which play a negative practical role in discouraging, criticizing, and blaming certain kinds of action, and guiding practical deliberation *via* internalized norms. And suppose also that they use "W" in such a way that it picks out a certain natural property of acts: namely, the property of detracting from the overall cohesion and strength of the group (as by weakening social bonds, wasting resources, etc.). Acts are condemned as W (i.e., as having the property of W-ness) when they involve deliberately or indifferently weakening group cohesion and strength, as by pursuing self-interest or the interest of those outside the group at the expense of the group's cohesion and strength. Those who deliberately or indifferently perform acts that are W are criticized, blamed, and punished, while those who avoid W acts are praised and held up as model citizens.

Given these assumptions, we have a naturalistic phenomenon involving a community's using a term and concept in a way that both (i) plays certain roles in regulating practical life, through internalized social norms involving praise and criticism, and (ii) picks out an objective, natural property that is ascribed to an act when it is claimed to be W. So, with these linguistic and behavioral practices in place, a certain class of acts may truly be said to be W, making for positive truths about W-ness; and at the same time, "W" is an ethical term and the concept and property of W-ness are ethical ones (given the practical roles they play). This means that we have *positive ethical truths* – indeed, *objective* ones since the property of W-ness is an objective property. And these ethical truths involve ontological commitment since W-ness is as much a part of the ontology of the world as any other natural property. Indeed, given that W-ness is a natural property, it will figure into *explanations* of empirical phenomena. We could cite an action's being W in explaining why people reacted to it in the way they did, or why it led to the demise of the group, and so on. This explanatory significance may seem to support the idea that we have *real ethical properties and facts* on the scene.[17]

Again, some might see this as vindicating ethical realism. For as long as we have managed to do something analogous with our own ethical language and thought, we need only identify the natural properties involved, after which it is a short step to establishing that many of our ordinary ethical claims are true. Suppose it turns out that we give "wrong" a practical role much like the one given to "W" by the community above, and we likewise use it to pick out a natural property. It looks like this property would then be the property of *wrongness*. This will likely be something more complex than W-ness – perhaps some "homeostatic cluster property" (Boyd 1997) or some massively disjunct-ive property (Jackson 1998), with disjuncts having to do with causing various harms, forms of suffering, offenses, and so on, in various possible circum-stances. Whatever the precise details, let's suppose that an act's being one of causing suffering for amusement makes it count as having this property of wrongness. In that case, ethical claims such as "Smith's making Jones suffer for amusement was wrong" turn out to be *objectively true* (assuming Smith did such a thing), correctly attributing an objective property to Smith's act. It might then seem that we have found a rather easy route to ethical realism.

Yet, we might now ask: Could anything that comes that easily really be capturing what we originally wanted in an ethical realism? There are a number of ways to bring out this worry. As a preliminary point before getting to the central issue in the next subsection, notice how thin the difference is between this sort of allegedly realist view and anti-realist or quasi-realist expressivism. Consider Allan Gibbard's view: despite being an expressivist who rejects realism, Gibbard grants that normative terms and concepts refer to real, natural properties. He takes the property of *being what ought to be done* to consist in a certain rather odd natural property: a massively disjunctive property corresponding to a "hyperplan" – that is, a property consisting in being an act of

---

[17] These ideas involving explanatorily significant natural ethical properties and facts are associated with "Cornell Realism," as developed by Sturgeon (1986, 1988, 2006), Brink (1989), and Boyd (1997). For doubts about the explanatory significance of such natural ethical properties, see Harman (1986).

type A1 in circumstances C1 (e.g., an act of jumping out the window when the building is on fire), or being an act of type A2 in circumstances C2, or . . .. and so on (Gibbard 2006, 324). This disjunctive property, he claims, is coextensive with and constitutes *being what one ought to do*. But this is on all fours *metaphysically* with the ethical naturalism endorsed by Frank Jackson (1998, 124). What primarily sets Gibbard's view apart from such ethical naturalism – or similarly from the naturalist realism about W-ness, and so on – is just Gibbard's rejection of representationalist *semantics*: he denies that normative claims *function to attribute* those natural properties to things (even though the concepts employed do refer to them); he argues that normative claims instead have a different, expressive function (Gibbard 2006, 324).[18]

We have a difference in semantics, then, but the ethical ontology is on a par, and in light of that, we might wonder: Are the semantic differences alone really getting at everything we were concerned with in seeking to carve out a distinctive theoretical space for ethical realism? Does the naturalist representationalist view sketched earlier really give us, just through such semantic and explanatory moves, something worth calling *objective ethical reality*?

For at least some of us, there is much more at stake in debates between realism and expressivism than just disagreements about how ethical language functions or precisely which mental states are expressed with ethical claims. (Indeed, expressivists such as Horgan and Timmons (2000, 2008) now agree that these mental states can be considered "beliefs," further closing the distance between the competing views – part of the "problem of creeping minimalism" articulated by Jamie Dreier 2004.) There seems to be something at stake that has not been captured merely by satisfying our four conditions so far.

2.2 The Underlying Problem

A more fundamental way to get at what is still missing is to notice the *contingency* in the concept/property pair adopted by a given community for purposes of social coordination *via* normative guidance – and the virtually limitless *alternatives* that could have been adopted instead. In our hypothetical example, we imagined a community focusing on the concept/property of foreseeably detracting from the overall cohesion and strength of the group, giving this a negative role in normative governance. But we could just as easily have

---

[18] He also denies that these natural properties are properly considered *normative properties*, even though they are the referents of normative concepts, that is, concepts with the relevant expressive practical role. This is because they are equally the referents of certain *non*normative concepts: We do not *require* normative concepts to characterize them, so there is nothing essentially normative about these properties.

picked any of an indefinitely large number of alternative concepts/properties, such as that of failing to maximize happiness or failing to maximally promote self-interest or the interests of one's kin group, or diminishing individual liberty – or some disjunctive concept/property with a vast number of disjuncts, creating still more room for variations by adding, dropping, or modifying various disjuncts.

The point, then, is that *if* one adopts the sort of model of ethical judgment and reference we have been considering so far in this section, then there seem to be myriad concept/property pairs to choose from, which could equally play the relevant practical roles in regulating social life, thus making for many different ethical concepts or properties (Eklund 2017). And this raises two important problems, which can be illustrated using the following hypothetical scenario:

> Suppose ten different linguistic/ethical communities have developed and adopted ten different sets of terms, concepts and corresponding properties to play these practical roles in their lives. Perhaps one is the community from earlier that uses "W" in negatively evaluating acts, and imagine (to consider now the positive flipside) that it uses "R" in positively evaluating acts, with R-ness being the property of *promoting* group cohesion and strength. The other nine have alternative terms, concepts and properties along the lines sketched earlier: "R1" and R1-ness, "R2" and R2-ness, and so on. One of these communities might be our own, as we employ "right" in parallel ways, with rightness perhaps being some complex disjunctive natural property picked out by "right" as we use it in our action-guiding norms and deliberation.

The first problem we can raise here has received substantial attention in the literature already in the form of worries about "Moral Twin Earth" scenarios (Horgan and Timmons 1991). On the model of ethical judgment and reference, we have been considering, each of these communities will be making *true ethical claims*, correctly attributing objective natural properties to acts – properties that count as "ethical" because they are the referents of terms and concepts with certain practical roles. But these properties will vary across communities: R-ness, R1-ness, rightness, and so on. So people in these different communities seem just to be *talking about different things*. We cannot translate one community's ethical terms (such as "R") using another's practically analogous term (such as "R1" or "right"), and we cannot interpret them as disagreeing about a common subject matter: they would simply be talking about different properties, where a given act could *both* possess the natural property that is rightness and yet lack the natural property that is R-ness, or vice versa. And yet, this seems like a deeply implausible take on what is going on across communities with different ethical judgments and practices. They instead seem typically to be addressing a common subject matter – *how it is appropriate to live* – and sometimes genuinely disagreeing about it, as when one endorses, and the other condemns one and the same act using their basic ethical concepts (Horgan and Timmons 1991).

The second problem, explored more recently by Matti Eklund (2017), is closely related but articulates an even more fundamental challenge for ethical realism. The focus here is a kind of *parity* worry about the alternatives. By giving us so many ethical properties and truths so easily, such an approach to ethical judgment and reference seems to make it impossible even to make sense of what is arguably the core idea of ethical realism: namely, that the *world itself, or reality, objectively favors certain ways of valuing and acting.* It might initially *seem* that we have captured that idea very well. After all, if rightness is some objective natural property of acts, then the world objectively determines which acts are truly right (and similarly, which are wrong): what is right or not is not up to us to decide, but is settled by how the world is so that the world in a sense tells us what constitutes right living. This sounds quite realist, doesn't it? But the problem is that exactly the same things can be said in connection with each of the other ten communities with respect to their analogous concepts and properties. Each of them may say, *equally correctly*, that the world settles or tells us what constitutes R living, or R1 living, and so on – the kind of living their system aims at in each case. All are so far entirely on a par.

This then raises the question: *what is to choose between these alternative normative schemes* – specifically in an *objective* way and not just trivially from within each framework in favor of itself? The world may settle which acts are R1, which are R2, and so on, each of these being used by different communities (including our own) to guide action as the referents of their respective ethical terms and concepts. But the world doesn't thereby say *which of these alternatives ought to be adopted* in the first place. Having adopted "right" and rightness to fill this role, we might feel that it is enough that there are objective facts about rightness since obviously *rightness* is what matters, not some other property such as R1-ness: we were interested in rightness, and once we've identified the property that is rightness, we're done. But the R1 community will of course just say something analogous, finding in favor of R1-ness rather than rightness, and similarly for all the other communities. And each remains so far *on a par* with all the others: nothing in our picture so far provides any resources for even giving a *sense* to the idea that one of these alternatives is *objectively correct* – the correct choice to make regarding which ethical concept/property to adopt and allow to shape our norms and govern our deliberations and how we live.

There is thus, so far, no intelligible sense for what it could even *be* for the world itself to favor one way of valuing and living over the other alternatives

(Eklund 2017). We may have "objective ethical truths" in some sense, but this has not actually gotten us very far, since if this is all there is to say then the world seems actually to be *silent* on how we are to value or live! All we have in this picture are various alternative concept/property pairs that can be given practical roles in regulating behavior via social norms: no sense has been given to the idea that any one choice among these alternatives is any more correct or incorrect than any other. Once we make a choice, certain claims within that framework will be objectively true or false: certain acts will or will not be R1, or R2, or right, and people can use certain claims to regulate behavior and correctly say that it is R1 to act a certain way, or right to act another way. But we seem so far to be at liberty to pick any of these schemes without making any kind of real mistake – and by the same token, without ultimately getting anything genuinely correct either, in terms of which way of valuing and living to adopt.

This seems more like a radical form of ethical *relativism* than like ethical realism. Although the above picture involves a kind of rejection of relativism in recognizing nonrelative facts about which acts possess R1-ness, and so on, at a deeper level, there is complete *parity* among these alternative systems, which may involve very different ways of valuing and acting. Ethical realism should deliver more than that.

It might be suggested that we can remedy this by appealing to practical *reasons*: if there are genuine reasons to care about and pursue *rightness* but not reasons to care about and pursue R1-ness or the other competing properties as such, then perhaps that could provide a sense in which the world favors organizing our practical lives around rightness rather than the alternative properties (cf. Schroeder 2005). There is indeed something promising in this idea. But the crucial point for now is that it will not in fact help *if* we continue to apply the present model of normative judgment and reference to account for objective truths about reasons since we will just run into the very same problem again.

Suppose someone claims that the property of being a reason is the objective natural property of being a consideration that helps make it the case that the action will serve goals associated with either rightness or prudence. On this proposal, the consideration that this wallet belongs to Jones, for example, plausibly has the property of *being a reason* to return it to her, since that consideration helps to make it the case that returning the wallet will serve goals associated with rightness, such as respecting property and mitigating distress. The problem, however, is that each of the other communities can analogously adopt *alternative* concept/property pairs similarly keyed to their analogues of rightness: one will employ the concept/property of being a reason1 (spelled out in terms of goals associated with R1), while another will employ the concept/property of being a reason2 (spelled out in terms of goals associated with R2), and so on. There will thus be objective facts about which considerations are reasons, and these will be related to objective facts about which actions are right. But in exactly the same way, there will likewise be a set of objective facts about which considerations are reasons1 that are related to objective facts about which actions are R1, and similarly for all the other alternatives.

We are thus back to the original *parity problem*, this time regarding reasons and analogue concepts/properties that are given analogous practical roles in other possible communities. Whatever underwriting the property of rightness receives by appealing to what there are reasons to value and pursue, alternative properties like R1-ness will receive parallel underwriting from analogues like reasons1. Nothing in this picture so far gives any special *normative authority* or status to one alternative over the others, except trivially in its own terms. We may feel like we've gotten somewhere because we can say that rightness is what really matters because, after all, there are genuine *reasons* to care about and pursue right action. But this is illusory because others can equally say that R1-ness is what really matters because, after all, there are genuine reasons1 to care about and pursue R1 actions, and so on for the rest. We have not yet succeeded in giving any sense at all to the idea that the world or reality itself favors one way of valuing and acting, for example, pursuing a life devoted to right action (as opposed to R1 action, etc.).

The lesson here is that in leaving room for so much contingency and parity, the approach we've been considering so far fails to give us much of anything we were likely after in speaking of an *objective ethical reality* in the first place. We already knew there were objective natural properties of the sort we've been talking about, having to do with an act's effects pertaining to harm, suffering, social stability, and so on. So it shouldn't be too surprising that merely telling a semantic story that allows terms and concepts with certain practical roles to pick out such properties, thus resulting in "objectively true ethical claims," fails to deliver what was desired. What ethical realists are properly after is a deeper kind of ethical objectivity that *eliminates the parity* we've described.

2.3 What Has Been Missing So Far

To get the deeper and more meaningful sort of ethical objectivity we're after we need an entirely different model from the one sketched earlier. If we were limited to that sort of model of ethical reference and properties then we might make sense of the very limited sort of objectivity described earlier, but we would have to give up on capturing the idea that reality itself objectively favors certain ways of valuing and acting over others. So if we are to do better on that front, we will need to rethink what is going on in ethical evaluation and what kinds of properties ethical properties might be.

To begin with, we need a different model for understanding evaluative concepts and properties. Although ethical concepts may be those to which we give certain practical roles, one of those roles is the *evaluation* of acts, character traits, persons, policies, and so on. And we do not have evaluation just by ascribing some mundane natural property in a way that is associated with the regulation of behavior and attitude. Evaluation involves something more complex than that, as we will see (even in cases where it is construed fully naturalistically). Expressivists will suggest that what needs to be added is some noncognitive element, such as a pro-attitude or disposition of choice toward anything evaluated as good. But in exploring realism, we are working on the representationalist assumption that evaluative claims are a matter of *attributing an evaluative property* to something. The question is then what exactly this attribution of an evaluative property, which consti- tutes evaluation in a realist framework, involves. And even in nonethical contexts, we can see that it involves something more than mere ascription of properties of the sort highlighted in the previous model.

Consider the evaluation of an artifact as good of its kind. This certainly involves the ascription of familiar natural properties to it in the course of attributing the evaluative property to it, as when we note that a knife is *sharp* and cuts neatly in the course of evaluating it as a *good* knife. But the evaluation of it as good is not simply the ascription of sharpness to it, nor is its being good simply the same thing as its being sharp. We can, after all, ascribe sharpness to a bookmark without thereby evaluating it as good, and it would not in fact be good by virtue of being sharp (indeed, a sharp bookmark is a bad one); we could likewise note that some artifact is sharp while not yet having any idea whether the thing is good or bad of its kind, if we're unfamiliar with this kind of thing – thus obviously not yet evaluating it one way or the other. The relation between sharpness and goodness in the knife is not one of identity, but a different sort of relation we flagged earlier: sharpness, in a knife, is a *good-making* property (while in a bookmark, it is a bad-making property). That is, sharpness is a feature that helps to make a knife satisfy the *standards* of excellence for knives, thereby making it a *good* knife (though it does the opposite in a bookmark with respect to standards for bookmarks).

To evaluate the knife as good is not simply to say that it is sharp, but to say something more complex: namely, that it possesses features, such as sharpness and rigidity, *by virtue of* which it satisfies the standards of excellence for knives, and so counts as a good knife. The evaluation essentially makes reference to relevant standards (though this is often implicit if they are obvious), and so does the characterization of the evaluative property. As a conceptual matter, the *evaluative property* – the goodness attributed to the knife, for example – will be the property the attribution of which (using the corresponding evaluative concept) *constitutes* evaluation. And as we have seen, this will be not merely a property like sharpness or rigidity as such, but the complex property of *having features that make the thing satisfy the relevant standards*. So the evaluative property is that complex property the characterization of which essentially makes reference to relevant evaluative standards.

In the case of a functional artifact like a knife, the standards are bound up with proper function, which is why features such as sharpness or rigidity count as good-making features of a knife: they make it satisfy relevant standards of excellence by making it function well for cutting (and there will be more specific functions and standards for particular kinds of knives). Since these background facts about function and standards can themselves presumably be accounted for naturalistically, the goodness of the knife is itself a natural property as well: the point here is just that it is not to be conflated with the good-making properties. (Whether evaluative properties in the ethical domain are likewise naturalistic is a further question we will take up later.)

In other cases, the standards may be fixed in other ways, but the same structural point applies: evaluation is not merely ascribing familiar features to something; it is attributing a distinct, *resultant evaluative property* to the thing, which it has *by virtue of* its possession of such features *and* the fact that they are good-making, that is, the fact that they make the thing satisfy relevant standards of excellence (Dancy 1993, 2004, 2006; cf. Parfit 2011). In evaluating something as good, we are not simply ascribing features that happen also to be good-making, but are ascribing them *as* good-making, which comes to the same as attributing the evaluative property of goodness to the thing, as such. (This is why one would obviously not be evaluating something just by attributing a good-making feature to it if one were not even aware that it was good-making.) It is this element of good-makingness or relation to relevant standards that is crucial to evaluation, whatever the source of the standards in question.

Returning to ethics, then, our task is to understand ethical evaluation, such as the claim that a certain character trait or action is good or right. Obviously, the source of standards of ethical goodness or rightness will not be the same as for artifacts, that is, facts about artificial functions.[19] But again, the same structural

---

[19] Some have proposed that *natural* functional teleology might serve as the basis for naturalistic and objective ethical norms (Foot 2001). This is discussed in Section 3.1. For a critique of teleological naturalism in ethics, see FitzPatrick (2000), and for a recent defense, see Moosavi (2019).

points apply. Just as we do not evaluate a knife or a bookmark as good simply in ascribing sharpness to it (even if sharpness is a good-*making* feature of a knife), we do not evaluate an act as right simply in ascribing to it an empirical property like being happiness maximizing. This is true even if it turns out that being happiness maximizing is the sole right-making property, so that acts are right if and only if they are happiness maximizing: there is still a distinction between merely ascribing a property like being happiness maximizing to an act and evaluating the act as right (cf. Parfit 2011). Nor does this distinction collapse just because we use a different term for the property of being happiness maximizing, to which we also give various practical roles (as with "R1," etc.). It is still not *evaluation* if we're just using other words to ascribe a property like being happiness maximizing as such; nor would this convert that property into an evaluative property (since again the latter would have to be a property the attribution of which constitutes evaluation).

As with the evaluation of artifacts, in order to be making a genuine evaluation of an act as right by (in part) ascribing a property such as being happiness maximizing, we need to be ascribing this property *as* right-making, and so we need to be making reference (at least implicitly) to relevant *standards* and the thing's *relations* to those standards by virtue of possessing those features. And the evaluative property, rightness, will again not simply be the property of being happiness maximizing (which is at most right-making), but the complex property of satisfying the relevant evaluative standards for action by virtue of having right-making properties such as that of being happiness maximizing. This is that complex property whose attribution constitutes evaluation. The evaluative fact that a certain act is right will have a similarly complex structure: it will not be identical to the fact that it is happiness maximizing even if that is a right-making fact about the act; instead, it will be the fact that the act has features that are right-making and thus satisfies relevant evaluative standards for action (FitzPatrick 2008, 2011, 2014a, 2018b, 2018c).[20]

None of this begs questions against ethical naturalism: for all we've said, rightness, like goodness in a knife, could turn out to be an entirely natural property if it turns out that ethical standards can be fully accounted for in some

---

[20] My claims here about the role played by relevant standards in evaluation or evaluative beliefs, and in evaluative properties and facts, is distinct from David Copp's (2007, ch. 5) claim – in articulating his "realist expressivism" –that moral evaluations or assertions not only express moral beliefs but also express, through conventional implicature, conative states consisting in subscription to a relevant set of standards (where this includes an intention to treat such standards as action-guiding). What I've said is consistent with that further claim about the pragmatics of moral assertion, which has a number of attractions, but my focus is on the implicit reference to standards in the content of moral beliefs themselves. The importance of this will become clear later.

purely naturalistic way (Copp 1995). The present point is just that the structural issues we've illuminated hold in the context of ethics no less than for artifacts. So even if ethical rightness turns out to be a natural property (and facts about rightness thus turn out to be natural facts), rightness must not be conflated with natural right-making properties such as being happiness maximizing or any of the natural properties considered earlier with the ten communities; it will have to be a more complex property that brings in relevant standards and relations.

These structural points about evaluation and evaluative properties and facts show that we need a different model of ethical discourse from the one described earlier. An ethical concept such as rightness is not simply one among indefinitely many concepts (such as R1, R2, etc.) that are used both to pick out particular natural properties and to play certain practical social roles in regulating behavior, attitudes and deliberation. Instead, the concept of rightness picks out a complex, resultant, evaluative property that can be characterized *formally*, that is, in a way that abstracts from any such particular natural properties, leaving it open which ones might turn out to be the right-making ones:

> Rightness is *the evaluative status an action can have by possessing (one or more of) whichever ordinary features turn out to be the right-making ones (and lacking counterbalancing wrong-making features), such that the act satisfies the appropriate evaluative standards for action.*

Because this formal characterization of rightness leaves it open which particular natural features of actions are right-making, communities with different ideas about this – and so different ideas about the content of the appropriate standards for human action – can all agree that they are at least talking about the same thing: rightness. It is not that one community is talking about one particular natural property, R1-ness, while another is talking about a different particular natural property, R2-ness, so that they are simply talking past one another and not even really disagreeing when they seem to be. Instead, they are all talking about the property of rightness as characterized just above and having genuine disagreements about the content of the appropriate evaluative standards for action (or equivalently, about which features of acts are right-making, or how exactly they interact and weigh against each other). This, therefore, avoids the first problem we ran into with the earlier, simpler model.

Most importantly, it likewise provides a way for realists to avoid the *parity problem*. The problem was that on the earlier semantic model and related assumptions about the kinds of properties in play, it was impossible even to give a sense to the idea that reality objectively favors one way of valuing and acting over others. We could not make sense of that idea because we lacked any means to articulate a sense in which the choice of one particular ethical concept/property pair over others could be objectively correct in any nontrivial sense, avoiding mere parity among the alternatives. But things change once we adopt the alternative model suggested here. Ethical evaluations, such as the attribution of rightness or wrongness to an act, are not merely ascriptions of some particular natural property or other to something: they involve essentially *normative* claims about *appropriate standards* and how the thing measures up in light of its features. We can have substantive ethical disagreements even where we agree on all the ordinary features of the act (e.g., whether or not it maximizes happiness or serves the interests of the group, etc.), since we can disagree about what the appropriate standards look like (or equivalently, which properties are the right-making ones). And this fact opens up precisely the space we need to finally make sense of the realist idea that has so far been eluding us. For if there can be substantive disagreement about what the appropriate standards are for evaluating human action, then there can in principle be a *fact of the matter* about which position in this disagreement is correct, thus eliminating the parity among competing views about rightness.[21]

Similar points apply to claims about reasons. If part of what we're trying to capture is the idea that ethics has *categorical normative authority* (it is not merely rationally optional), then we need to be able to claim that a certain set of standards is the objectively appropriate one not only for evaluating human action but likewise for governing human deliberation and conduct: it provides the proper target for us to aim at in practical life, appropriately guiding and settling deliberation. This is how to understand the claim that there is genuine *reason* to live according to a certain set of ethical standards. Just as talk of rightness is not merely talk of an empirical property such as being happiness maximizing, talk of something's being a reason for acting is likewise not merely talk of some related empirical property (such as being a consideration that helps to make it the case that the action will advance either overall happiness or self-interest) – as imagined earlier, which saddled us with the parity problem. To make normative claims about practical reasons is to make claims about *which kinds of considerations appropriately guide and settle deliberation*. This is the analogue for reasons of the formal characterization of rightness above.

On this model, then, people with different substantive views about reasons can again all be talking about the same thing, characterized normatively and abstractly, and disagree about it, rather than simply talking past each other. And again, if there can be a substantive disagreement about what appropriately guides and settles deliberation, then there can in principle be a fact of the matter about which position in this disagreement is correct. We thus arrive finally at

---

[21] This is obviously not yet to argue for the existence of such a fact of the matter, which we will turn to in Section 4. The point is just that we now have the resources – to be further developed in Section 3 – to make sense of the realist idea that requires getting past the parity situation.

what the realist needs to posit in order to capture the desired thoughts about objective ethical reality – namely, a *normative fact* along the following lines:

> **NF**: The world, or reality, is such that a certain set of standards (rather than indefinitely many others) is in fact the objectively appropriate or proper one for ethically evaluating and governing human practical life.

If there is such a normative fact, over and above all the mundane facts about the empirical properties of actions, then we finally have a clear sense in which *reality itself favors one way of valuing and acting over others*.

For example, if reality contains normative facts about human dignity, which in turn ground a set of ethical standards involving respect for persons as the inherently appropriate response to the dignity we encounter in them, then this set of standards would be *underwritten by reality*. They would be at least part of the set of standards that is genuinely and objectively appropriate for evaluating and governing practical life – unlike standards that fail to find any such objective grounding in reality. Reality itself would favor valuing, deliberating, and acting in accordance with standards springing from human dignity.

To posit such an objective ethical reality is a very different thing from merely positing a plethora of alternative mundane concepts and properties that might be given practical roles, as imagined with the earlier communities that were ultimately *on a par*, none any more "aligned with reality itself" than the others. I have suggested that such parity is in fact deeply inconsistent with the true spirit of ethical realism. Those of us who wish to be realists *about ethics* in a full-blooded way aspire to more than just some way of getting some positive ethical claims to come out true with worldly and objective truth-makers. As we saw earlier, that meager aim can be achieved in ways that leave reality strikingly indifferent to how we live our lives. We aspire to an objective ethical reality that favors certain ways of valuing and living over others, as articulated by NF (and brought out in the fifth claim).

The impression that ethics involves this sort of categorical correctness and normative authority is not just a preoccupation of certain realists. Neo-Kantian constructivists agree on this point, ironically being much closer in this respect to realists who accept NF than are fellow realists who embrace only the first four claims. The difference is just that neo-Kantians attempt to account for such categoricity in a nonrealist fashion, as described earlier. Realists are skeptical that Kantians can pull that rabbit out of the hat of mere agency, but if a realist who embraces NF were to lose confidence that it can be given a realist account, she might sooner turn to a view like neo-Kantianism and attempt to make it work than settle for a deflationary form of realism that accepts the earlier parity.

Nor are neo-Kantians the only allies in holding that ethics is bound up with a deep objectivity involving categorical normative authority. Even error theorists grant that the idea captured by NF is bound up with ethical concepts and judgments – this being precisely what they take to be the source of error in ethics since they deny the truth of NF (Mackie 1977; Joyce 2002). If ethics did not include this claim of categoricity or "objective prescriptivity" then there would be no such error by their lights; however, ethics would also be much less interesting and metaethically controversial! As Mackie was well aware, it is easy enough to generate true normative claims that are merely relativized to a stipulated set of standards that one is free to take or leave, as when judging pies at the county fair (or similarly, relativized to a set of standards that objectively meets some similarly stipulated criterion for justification). But ethics on that model is so innocuous as not to be worth targeting. Error theorists would never have bothered rejecting traditional ethical discourse as riddled with error if they saw it as making only such relativized claims, or claims to truth of the sort imagined earlier with various communities using expressions with practical roles to talk about natural properties. Instead, error theorists target typical ethical discourse precisely because they see it as building in much more.

Similarly, though she is not an error theorist, Sharon Street (2008a) has emphasized that her evolutionary debunking argument is meant to target the kind of realism that is "worth worrying about," that is, realism that incorporates such categoricity. And finally, expressivists also recognize the element of categorical normative authority built into ethical judgment: the difference is again just that they propose to account for this in a nonrealist way, in this case using an expressivist model of normative judgment (Horgan and Timmons 2018). As with neo-Kantians, this makes them in some ways closer to the present sort of realist than are realists who reject NF; and again, someone who gives up on the more ambitious realism (perhaps due to metaphysical qualms) might sooner turn to a sophisticated expressivism than to a form of realism that rejects NF.[22]

Realists who embrace NF are therefore in good company in seeing ethics as aspiring to more than the kind of objective truth we were left with at the end of Section 1, and I have tried to show in any case that the spirit of ethical realism pushes us beyond those first four conditions, to the more full-blooded view of objective ethical reality we have sketched here. So although we won't build in the following claim as a strict condition for a view's counting as "realist,"

---

[22] This is perhaps illustrated by Parfit's (2017, 64) ultimate affinity for something close to expressivist quasi-realism, which he regards as "another form of Non-Realist Cognitivism."

I propose that we add a fifth claim that will at least be embraced by what I take to be a proper paradigm of ethical realism:

> (5) **Favoring by Reality Itself**: Among the objective features of the world or reality are some that make it the case that "reality itself favors certain ways of valuing and acting" over others (Eklund 2017, 1), such that a certain set of ethical standards (rather than indefinitely many others) is in fact the objectively appropriate or proper one for ethically evaluating and governing human practical life.

The addition of this condition gives us the view I will call "ardent ethical realism."[23] This takes us beyond what is secured by the first four conditions. By adding claim 5, we eliminate the sort of parity that plagued us earlier and articulate a deeper and more robust notion of objective ethical reality that plausibly belongs at the very heart of ethical realism.[24]

3 Ardent Ethical Realism and the Value-Laden World

We have now arrived at what I take to be paradigmatic ethical realism, characterized by five central claims developed in the previous two sections:

(1) **Representational Content**: about the semantics of ethical discourse;
(2) **Truth**: about the existence of positive ethical truths;
(3) **Stance-Independence**: about the relevant independence or objectivity of those truths;
(4) **Ontological Commitment**: about the ontological commitment implied by ethical truths;
(5) **Favoring by Reality Itself**: about the world's having features that make a certain set of ethical standards the objectively appropriate or proper standards for ethically evaluating and governing human practical life so that reality itself favors certain ways of valuing and acting.

---

[23] Though I borrow the expression "ardent realism" from Eklund (2017), his concern is with ardent normative realism in a sense that doesn't necessarily imply ethical realism, while I understand "ardent ethical realism" to encompass realism about morality, reasons, and other aspects of ethics broadly speaking.

[24] As noted in Section 1.3, I am skeptical that we can make sense of the special status of the correct ethical standards (as articulated in claim 5) by construing them as a set of *conceptual* truths (Cuneo and Shafer-Landau 2014). There are lots of concepts and related conceptual truths that could be used to regulate life, but the question is why we should embrace one rather than another – for example, *rightness* (with the specific content Cuneo and Shafer-Landau see as built into it as the "moral fixed points") rather than *honor* (in the sense related to brutal "honor killings" associated with deeply sexist ideologies). Claim 5 (as developed further in Section 3) provides a way of answering that question: The point will be that the standards associated with the former are grounded in irreducibly normative aspects of the world, while the standards associated with the latter have no such grounding.

Since we have already discussed the first four claims in detail, it is worth now saying more about the fifth to fill out the notion of ardent ethical realism. What exactly is it that we are positing in making this claim, and how exactly could the world be that way?[25]

3.1 An Irreducibly Normative Claim and Fact

The fact posited in claim 5 is a *normative* one, about there being features of the world that make it inherently *appropriate* for us to employ a certain set of standards in ethical evaluation and rational deliberation, organizing our lives as rational agents around these standards. And given the commitment to stance-independence in claim 3, this fact is not to be accounted for in any stance-dependent way, as on constructivist attempts to reduce it to something about what we would desire or approve of or be motived by under certain conditions. It is supposed to be a stance-independent, objective fact about the world and its ramifications. In fact, not only is reduction to idealized subjective facts ruled out but as I will now argue, so apparently is any reduction to stance-independent, objective facts that can (at least in principle) be characterized in *non*normative, merely descriptive terms. For it is hard to see how any such facts could capture the realist thought in claim 5.

Suppose someone proposes reducing the normative fact asserted in 5 to an empirical, nonnormative fact (one that can be fully spelled out in nonnormative terms), such as:

> **H**: a certain set of ethical standards is such that if people adopted and followed it this would maximize total happiness as measured by a certain psychological theory of happiness.

The problem is that such a reduction just obliterates the intended content of the claim in 5 – that is, that these are the standards it is objectively appropriate for us to organize our practical lives around – rather than capturing it in other terms. H may be *relevant* to the normative fact asserted by 5, but it is not *the same fact*. There are, after all, any number of empirical facts about the personal or social consequences of adopting certain standards, among other things, but none of them is *itself* the normative fact asserted by 5. Indeed, any attempt to make such an identification would just land us right back in the earlier parity problem, defeating the whole point of claim 5. At most, it might be the case that one of these empirical facts, such as H, can be used to *support* the claim in 5 *when combined with relevant normative claims*.

---

[25] Some of the ideas in this section are also explored in FitzPatrick (Forthcoming).

For example, we might add to H the normative claims:

(i) that happiness, and only happiness (as construed by the psychological theory in question), is intrinsically valuable,

(ii) that practical reason is properly concerned with maximizing value, and thus that

(iii) maximizing overall happiness is the proper or appropriate aim of practical reason – that is, the aim internal to proper exercises of practical reasoning – appropriately guiding and settling rational deliberation for us (as opposed to alternatives such as maximally promoting self-interest, or desire-satisfaction, or in-group cohesion or power, or creative accomplishment, etc.).

If this set of normative claims were added to the empirical claim H, this would perhaps establish claim 5 in connection with this set of standards: it might imply that there are objective features of reality, that is, happiness and practical reason, which (given facts about their value and proper aim, respectively) make it the case that reality itself favors valuing and acting according to the standards that, when adopted and followed, maximize that happiness.

The point, though, is that this normative fact (a version of 5) is not identical with H and was derived from H only through the addition of a set of claims that *remain normative* – claims about the intrinsic value of happiness and its being the proper aim or target of practical reason, appropriately guiding and settling practical deliberation. And for similar reasons, there is no plausible reduction of those claims to any *non*normative objective and stance-*independent* claims that would still yield the desired content of claim 5. We seem here to need to fall back on some *ineliminably normative* claims in accounting for 5, either taking 5 as itself a fundamental normative claim or deriving it partly from more fundamental normative claims (not merely from claims like H).

Some might instead seek a different reduction of claim 5 that captures its content while avoiding ineliminably normative claims. A certain kind of neo-Aristotelian might appeal here to an application of the normativity bound up with natural teleological facts about living things. There seem to be objective facts about proper functions associated with organs such as hearts or eyes, which provide objective standards for evaluating a given organ's structure and functioning as normal or defective. And the same is true for natural teleological facts and norms associated with higher levels of functioning involving perception, psychology, and behavior – facts about proper functions and standards pertaining to a lioness's hunting, or a bird's nest-building, or a gazelle's fleeing a predator. If there are such teleological facts pertaining to higher levels of human life as well, including the operations of practical reason and choice – the sphere of ethics – then perhaps these facts yield objective standards for evaluating human character traits, deliberation, and action. Such facts might thus underwrite the appropriateness of those standards, just as in the case of the eye (Foot 2001). Someone might then suggest that claim 5 can be reduced to:

> **T**: A certain set of ethical standards is such that it aligns with standards rooted in objective, natural teleological facts about proper human functioning at this level.

On many views of natural teleology, facts about proper functions and ends underlying the normative facts can be accounted for without reliance on any ineliminably normative claims. The normative fact that a given eye is defective in the way it focuses images would be based on standards associated with facts about proper function for the eye; and the latter might be reductively accounted for by appeal to the natural selection causal history that shaped the eye in connection with a special subset of effects (such as focusing light in beneficial ways), providing a sense of what it is "designed" to do (as on consequence-etiological accounts, such as Wright 1976). Similarly with functional psychological and behavioral traits in animals, including humans. So if some such reduction of natural teleology is successful, then it might seem that we can capture the idea in 5 without commitment to ineliminable normativity in the world.

This appearance, however, is again illusory. The claims about natural teleology and related norms may well establish that there is a kind of objective, function-based normative framework applicable to living things, allowing for species-relative normative standards supporting a related kind of normative judgment. It might even be true that this framework can be applied to higher levels of human life. Elsewhere, I have argued that there are indeed objective biological teleological facts associated with all evolved organisms at all levels of functioning that have been influenced by a natural selection causal history, including human psychology and behavior (FitzPatrick 2000). There is, however, a fundamental gap between this claim and the ardent realist claim in 5. The teleologically based claim tells us that there is a natural teleological normative framework that can be applied to human life *for purposes of assessing proper biological functioning* – for example, in making claims about a certain behavior's being defective with respect to biological functional standards. It requires a crucial further step, however, to get to the claim in 5, that these biological functional standards (in connection with the relevant sphere of human life) are the ones that are appropriate for *ethical* evaluation and governance, providing *an authoritative standard that merits our fundamental concern and devotion as rational agents.*

Why, after all, should we as autonomous, rational agents care in the least whether some action turns out to be defective as judged by natural teleological standards rooted in facts about our evolutionary history or any other set of nonnormative facts that might ground the teleological facts? This question isn't answered for us by the mere fact that those teleological standards apply to us for certain limited evaluative purposes: the question is why they should be given the elevated role of governing our practical lives. I have elsewhere argued that on a plausible, rigorous account of natural teleology, it quickly becomes clear that such standards would be wildly inappropriate candidates for ethical ones (FitzPatrick 2000). But the main point here is about the *normative gap* in any case: in order for T to provide any support for claim 5, we would again need to add a supplementary normative claim:

> The objective biological teleological standards associated with human life are the ones that it is *appropriate for us, as rational and moral agents, to use for ethical purposes, organizing our lives around them and using them to settle our deliberations*.

Setting aside the inherent implausibility of that claim, the real point is that it is a further normative claim that would be needed in such an undertaking, just as we saw was needed with claim H. The natural teleological story, even if granted as far as it goes in establishing the existence of teleological standards that can correctly be applied to human life, does not *itself* give us that crucial normative claim; and without that, we don't get anything like claim 5. So this approach would still need to fall back on a supplemental normative claim.

There is, of course, room for further argument here, but I believe the above reflections on H and T strongly suggest that the fact we are after with claim 5 cannot be characterized nonnormatively or established without reliance on normative claims: if we try to do either we just seem to leave behind the very fact we were trying to capture, substituting in some other fact that does not do the work the ardent realist is after with claim 5. In other words, the fact posited in 5 seems to be an *irreducibly normative fact*, that is, one that can be properly characterized only in normative terms because of its inherently normative nature, and seems to be either fundamental or grounded in a set of facts that are likewise normative, such as the facts about inherent fittingness discussed in Section 3.3 (cf. FitzPatrick 2008, 2011, 2014a, 2018b, 2018c; Enoch 2011; Parfit 2011, 2017; Scanlon 2014).[26]

---

[26] It is important to understand that this goes beyond merely claiming that ethical *concepts* are irreducibly normative. Even expressivists grant that ethical concepts are irreducibly normative, while of course denying the existence of worldly properties and facts having an inherently normative nature (Gibbard 2006). The argument above is that we seem to need to posit the latter to avoid parity problems. This is because the fact posited in claim 5 seems to be either fundamental or explicable only via other normatively characterized properties and facts (as further spelled out in Section 3.3): They are not even *in principle* explicable by appeal to clusters of scientific properties and facts or (nonnormatively characterizable) functional roles played by them, and so on. Merely positing irreducibly normative *concepts* will not get us what the ardent realist needs to escape parity problems.

We can therefore add a further claim for ardent ethical realism:

> (6) **Irreducibly Normative Reality**: There are at least some *irreducibly normative properties and facts*, which (given claims 4 and 5) are *worldly* (part of reality) and so *ontologically* robust, and either fundamental or grounded partly in more fundamental normative properties and facts, such that there is normative reality "all the way down."[27]

3.2 Ethical Naturalism or Nonnaturalism?

What does this sixth claim mean for the metaethical debate between naturalistic and nonnaturalistic versions of ethical realism? That will depend on how we understand these categories. Naturalistic ethical realism posits only a naturalistic ontology and takes ethical properties and facts to be included among natural properties and facts. But how are the latter delimited? There is disagreement about this, but a fairly workable idea is that natural properties or facts are those that are in principle empirically investigable by the natural and social sciences or at least constructible from and exhaustively constituted by properties and facts that are. The latter allows for complex natural properties that figure into ethical discourse but are not themselves subjects of scientific investigation (Sturgeon 2006).

On this understanding, the property of being happiness maximizing would count as a natural one, right alongside the properties scientists investigate. So would the sort of massively disjunctive property considered earlier or a complex property consisting of a cluster of natural properties of ethical relevance. Some ethical naturalists maintain a "non-reductionist ethical naturalism," where this means that the complex natural properties they believe are picked out by ethical terms or concepts such as "goodness" or "rightness" may not be ones for which we have any ready nonethical terms or concepts (Sturgeon 2006). Even if ethical naturalism is true, there needn't exist any such reductive formula as: rightness = being happiness maximizing. Indeed, this lack of reduction of properties picked out by ethical terms to any properties picked out by existing nonethical terms would nicely explain G. E. Moore's well-known Open Question phenomenon (Moore 1903). That is, it would explain why, for any such identification Moore considered, there always seemed to be room for doubt among competent speakers about whether an action that had the nonethically characterized property really thereby had the ethically characterized one

---

[27] Unless otherwise specified, "normative" is meant to be understood broadly, encompassing both the evaluative (e.g., goodness, rightness) and the normative more narrowly construed (reasons, oughts, facts about what is appropriate or proper, and so on). Irreducibly normative properties and facts are those that cannot be characterized except in some such normative terms, or accounted for without appeal to some such normative properties and facts.

(e.g., "sure, this act would be happiness maximizing, but is it really *right*?") One might expect such gaps or open questions about any purported identification of this sort even if ethical properties were natural ones, as long as they were complex enough to resist the reductive treatment needed for the sorts of formulas Moore considered and found problematic (Sturgeon 2003, 2006).[28]

We've already seen why ardent ethical realists, at any rate, would find even such "non-reductionist" naturalistic views unsatisfactory: despite the non-reductionist naturalist's rejection of *formulaic reduction*, there is still ultimately a reduction of *the evaluative or the normative* to properties and facts that could at least in principle be fully characterized in nonevaluative/nonnormative terms, since they are simply constructed from and exhaustively constituted by mundane properties that can be so characterized. There is, on that picture, *no irreducibly evaluative or normative reality* on the scene: just ordinary empirical properties, perhaps grouped in complex ways, for which we have certain special terms and concepts that we give special practical and perhaps explanatory roles. That does not get us anything like the ardent realist's claim 5, which involves a deeper sort of irreducibility (to avoid the parity problem): namely, irreducibly normative properties and facts in the world, which cannot *even in principle* be properly captured or characterized in nonnormative terms and are not simply constructs of ordinary empirical properties or exhaustively constituted by them.

On the characterization of the naturalist/nonnaturalist distinction sketched earlier, the ardent realist therefore comes out as an ethical nonnaturalist or nonnaturalist ethical realist. This is indeed the standard way of characterizing "robust" ethical realism (FitzPatrick 2008; Enoch 2011). But the only reason metaphysical "nonnaturalism" has entered the picture is that we have posited *irreducibly normative* properties and facts in order to capture the idea in claim 5: there is no other sense in which we have had to embrace a "nonnaturalist metaphysics." Nonnaturalist realism is often caricatured as gratuitously embracing mysterious or "spooky" nonnatural properties. Allan Gibbard (2003, 16), for example, uses the nonsense term "exnat" as an empty placeholder for whatever this strange nonnatural property might turn out to be, and Frank Jackson (1998, 127) is mystified by the idea that any such strange metaphysical addition could possibly do any real work in ethics. But that is a misunderstanding of the role of nonnaturalism. We are not trotting out some new, obscure property like "exnat,"

---

[28] Moore framed his Open Question Argument in terms of goodness rather than rightness, rejecting the identification of goodness with properties such as being desired to be desired. Oddly, he didn't deploy a parallel argument against the identification of rightness with the property of maximizing goodness of consequences, though as deontologists emphasize, there is similar room for doubt about whether something that caused the best overall consequences was really morally right.

divorced from our ethical concepts, to do mysterious work (as Gibbard suggests by calling nonnaturalism "mumbo jumbo," 2003, 192). All we are doing is making a familiar normative claim about a set of ethical standards – that it is the appropriate one for ethical evaluation and for guiding human deliberation and action – and then maintaining that this claim states an irreducibly normative truth about the world, that is, a truth that cannot be explicated in nonnormative terms because it is *about* something *inherently normative*.

Indeed, once we see that the "nonnaturalistic" element of such a view just comes down to the inclusion of irreducibly normative properties and facts in our ontology, we might wonder why it should have been assumed in the first place that the natural world must exclude such things, consigning them to some other realm. This was really just an artifact of thinking of the natural world as limited to properties and facts that are either transparent to scientific investigation or exhaustively constituted by those that are. But why think that natural reality is exhausted by such properties and facts? That scientistic assumption creates the impression that only what is transparent to scientific investigation (or constructible from things that are) really belongs to the natural world in which we live so that anything else is either unreal or belongs to some other, mysterious, "nonnatural" realm. But there is another way to approach all of this.

We might say instead that there is a *single* world or reality, with which we are intimately familiar and which may as well be called "the natural world"; but scientific investigation (along with philosophical extensions building on it) is not the only way we engage with and know about that world: it has aspects we engage with and learn about in other ways, as through lived ethical experience. These may include evaluative or normative aspects of the same reality we also engage with scientifically but which we learn about as ethical agents – things such as the intrinsic badness of suffering, or the intrinsic worth or dignity of persons, and the objective normative significance each of these has for deliberation, that is, the reasons they give us for acting. On this picture, these are evaluative or normative aspects of the same things – suffering or persons – that we can *also* investigate scientifically, but they are not in any way reducible to the features we learn about scientifically (or constructs of such things): they are irreducibly evaluative or normative features we grasp in the course of engaged ethical agency (FitzPatrick 2008). Calling these "nonnatural" may misleadingly suggest that they belong to some other realm, which doesn't follow from the fact that they present in ways that are not transparent to scientifically based inquiry and have an evaluative or normative nature. It might actually be less misleading just to expand our conception of *the natural* to include all the sorts of worldly properties and facts we encounter, whether through scientifically based inquiry or in ethical life. There is *one reality*, the natural world, that happens to be ontologically rich enough to include inherently evaluative and normative aspects of things as well as scientifically transparent ones.

Interestingly, this parallels a move some have made in the philosophy of mind (FitzPatrick 2018a). It is often assumed that the physical world is limited to the properties and facts investigable by (or constructible from those investigable by) physics through its objective empirical methods. On that understanding, the physical world includes properties and facts pertaining to neural structures and dynamics or functions, for example, but would not include irreducibly phenomenal properties and facts, such as *qualia* or facts about what it is like to see blue; such properties or facts – which seem neither discoverable through physics nor derivable from facts about physical entities and laws – would be excluded from the physical and labeled "non-physical." But some, pursuing ideas developed by Bertrand Russell (1927), reject that approach, opting for a broader understanding of the physical that is not constrained by what is discoverable through objective empirical methods, that is, the "structure and dynamics" explored by physics, but includes further intrinsic properties of that world (see Alter and Nagasawa 2015 for discussion).

Those who take this approach maintain that the very same world of matter and energy investigated by physics may also contain intrinsic properties and facts that are irreducibly phenomenal in nature and thus present in a different way – not to scientific instruments, in the way that facts about the structure and dynamics of neurons do, but directly to a conscious subject of experience (Strawson 2015). Irreducibly phenomenal or experiential reality, on this view, is no less part of the one physical world we inhabit than are the kinds of properties and facts accessible to physics. Phenomenal or experiential reality is not part of some "otherworldly realm"; it is just a part of reality that doesn't reduce to the other parts and is known directly through subjective experience rather than through objective empirical investigation – as we know what it is like to see blue *by seeing blue* rather than by physically examining neurons in the brain of someone who is seeing blue.

There are many complications here, and the point of this parallel is not to suggest that we can answer metaphysical and epistemological questions in ethics simply by importing models from the philosophy of mind. Still, the parallels between the irreducibly normative reality posited by ardent ethical realists and the irreducibly phenomenal reality posited by some philosophers of mind are suggestive. In both cases, there is some striking aspect of reality that we are resistant to either eliminating or deflating through ontological reduction to something else that might fit more comfortably into a familiar scientific worldview. There is likewise a resistance to accepting a narrow, scientifically constrained understanding of the natural or physical world, according to which anything that doesn't fit into such a conception must belong to some other, suspect realm.

On the proposed alternative, the ardent ethical realist can be an ethical naturalist after all, on a broad understanding of the natural that does not exclude the irreducibly evaluative or normative, so that ethical properties and facts can be natural *without* being reduced to *other* natural properties and facts (or even complex clusters of such properties and facts) that are *not* irreducibly normative in nature. In any case, what I have tried to bring out here is that the metaethical debate between ethical naturalists and ethical nonnaturalists really just comes down to a debate over whether or not there is irreducibly normative reality. If a sufficiently expansive, "Non-Scientistic Naturalism" (FitzPatrick 2018a) can incorporate such a thing, then this metaphysical debate collapses: even the most ardent realist can enter the naturalist camp at that point. This suggests that the focus of debate in this area should really shift from an abstract discussion of naturalist vs. nonnaturalist metaphysics to focus just on *whether there is irreducible normativity in the world* (and not just in our concepts), and how it might be understood.

3.3 More on the Core Claim: Worldly Values, Practical Reason, and Fittingness

We have said that ardent ethical realists are committed to the following claim:

> (5) **Favoring by Reality Itself**: Among the objective features of the world or reality are some that make it the case that "reality itself favors certain ways of valuing and acting" over others (Eklund 2017, 1), such that a certain set of ethical standards (rather than indefinitely many others) is in fact the objectively appropriate or proper one for ethically evaluating and governing human practical life.

I have argued that this likewise commits them to the existence of irreducibly normative properties and facts, as articulated in claim 6: that is, claim 5 seems to be irreducibly normative in the sense that it can only be framed in normative terms, and any adequate account of its truth will likewise involve ineliminably normative claims (rather than potentially bottoming out in something about merely empirical properties and facts). In Section 3.1, we looked at some examples of how one might give a sense to this idea of reality's *objective favoring* of a certain set of ethical standards by supplementing claims like H or T with certain normative claims. I don't believe either of those examples is promising, however, so I will now suggest a better way to understand this general idea and begin filling it out.

The idea that reality itself objectively favors a certain set of standards as the proper one for ethically evaluating and governing human practical life can be understood in terms of two related *fittingness* claims. The first is this:

> (7) **Objectively Fitting Standards**: There are features of reality with an irreducibly normative nature that consists partly in making certain responses to those features *inherently fitting* or *unfitting*. Such features may thus be understood to ground a certain set of standards for feeling, choice, and action as the set that is *aligned with normative reality*, by virtue of articulating *inherently fitting responses* to these features as they are encountered (in various circumstances and combinations) in practical life.[29]

This asserts that a certain set of ethical standards is set apart from other candidates by the fact that it is built around capturing what it is to live in a way that befits *normative reality by realizing inherently fitting responses to real normative properties and facts* – where the normative nature or content of those properties and facts fixes such facts about fittingness. The world is *inherently value-laden* in certain ways, with implications, via fittingness relations, for the content of objectively appropriate ethical standards.

For example, suppose suffering is a feature of reality with irreducibly normative significance insofar as it is intrinsically bad. (This is not to deny that some suffering has instrumental value, such as pain from a broken limb that protects against further injury. It is also not to deny that some forms of suffering are morally appropriate responses to circumstances, as with grief over the loss of a loved one, such that it would be better to suffer that grief *given* those circumstances than not to feel it. The point is that all else being equal, suffering in and of itself is bad.) Part of what that entails is that it would be an unfitting response to suffering to be indifferent to it or an unfitting relation to it to cause it carelessly or to deliberately exacerbate it. Given the evaluative or normative aspects of suffering, it is inherently fitting, all else being equal, to seek to avoid causing it, and to mitigate it when we encounter it. These facts about fittingness would then inform ethical standards by grounding prescriptions of fitting responses to suffering and proscriptions against unfitting ones. If we frame ethical standards in virtue-theoretic terms, for example, such facts would partly ground the virtues of beneficence and non-maleficence filling out some of their content.

---

[29] The notion of inherently fitting or unfitting responses plays an important role in the account of moral *phenomenology* defended by Horgan and Timmons (2008), though they depart from the ardent realist by denying that fittingness or unfittingness are real properties or relations instantiated in the world. In FitzPatrick (2021), I argue that their cognitivist expressivist account does not succeed in fully capturing the moral phenomenology in question, which instead requires a realist ontology along the lines developed here.

Similarly, suppose rational nature or personhood is a feature of reality with irreducibly normative significance, bearing intrinsic worth or dignity. Part of what that would entail is that there are inherently fitting or unfitting ways of relating to persons as beings possessed of such worth or dignity. The details will of course depend on how exactly we flesh out the notion of dignity in first-order ethical theory, but it would plausibly be inherently unfitting (a violation of dignity) to treat persons as mere means to one's ends, disregarding their autonomy, or otherwise treating them as if they or their well-being mattered less than they do, as in carelessly subjecting them to harm and violating rights associated with dignity. Instead, a fitting response to persons, in light of their dignity and as part of what dignity entails, requires treating them as ends in themselves, with the recognition respect bound up with that value. Again, if we think of ethical standards in virtue-theoretic terms, such facts would partly ground the virtues of justice and respect, and fill out some of their content.

Ethical standards built on facts about fitting responses to normative aspects of reality would thus be aligned with normative reality in a way that gives a clear sense to the notion that reality itself favors these standards (by contrast with proposed standards that are not similarly grounded in normative features of reality). But we still need to say more to capture the idea that this objectively favored set of standards would also be one we have good reason to take seriously as *normatively authoritative* for us, properly governing our practical lives. After all, as we saw in Section 3.1, there might be a set of standards that is in some sense objectively in accord with certain aspects of reality but which we, as autonomous rational agents, have no reason to take seriously as having any claim to govern our behavior. (In the case of T, for example, we could reasonably ask: Who cares if certain behaviors would be in accordance with standards associated with evolutionarily based facts about natural teleology in human life?) So we need to add a further normative claim here about the nature of *practical reason* that would secure this connection. In particular, we need a normative claim about practical reason and the kinds of considerations that appropriately settle deliberation for an autonomous rational agent, thus constituting genuine reasons for acting, to capture the idea of genuine normative authority. And this would then have to connect up suitably with claim 7.

This would require extensive argument to support fully, but the basic line of thought can be sketched as follows (which will bring us to our eighth and final claim). First, in thinking about what the *appropriate standards* governing practical reason might look like, we need to start by thinking about the nature of practical reason itself. The key idea here is that practical reason is a robust capacity that is not limited in its operations merely to deliberation seeking instrumentally efficient means to given ends, or oriented toward some narrow and specific target such as satisfying our desires or maximizing our self-interest or following some conventional set of norms. As rational deliberators, we are not limited to framing our deliberation narrowly with questions such as "what will most efficiently serve my goals?" or "what will best satisfy my desires or interests or cohere with my society's norms?" and so on. Instead, we are capable of posing a broader and more fundamental question from a maximally comprehensive and critical evaluative deliberative perspective, namely,

> **Comprehensive Deliberative Question**: What would it be *all-things-considered good* for me to do, constituting *acting well* without qualification, here and now, given my total circumstances?

This most fundamental and comprehensive deliberative question incorporates all the other more specific questions, since it allows open input from facts about desire-satisfaction, self-interest, goals, social norms, and so on, in the course of determining how it would be all-things-considered good for one to act in one's circumstances. But deliberation driven by the fundamental, comprehensive question refracts these various considerations through this lens emphasizing all-things-considered goodness of action or acting well, rather than simply aiming at desire-satisfaction or the promotion of self-interest *as such*.

Now, if our faculty for practical cognition were instead limited to specific forms of deliberation about satisfying one's desires or promoting one's interests as such, then nothing more could reasonably be expected from it than sound instrumental reasoning geared toward these specific targets (and we would of course not even count as moral agents). If there are any appropriate standards for a practical faculty with that limited, parochial nature (beyond the biological teleological ones associated with constituent evolved traits), they would have to be standards suited to that limited nature. Such a faculty, we might say, would thus have as its *proper aim/concern/target* nothing more than desire-satisfaction, as on neo-Humean accounts, or self-interest maximization, as on egoist accounts: that's all that exercises of such a faculty would aim at when functioning properly according to those standards, and criteria for *success* in such exercises would be similarly focused and limited. Perhaps this actually applies to certain primates or to some of our hominin ancestors.

Since our faculty of practical reason has the more sophisticated nature we've described, however, involving a capacity for comprehensive, critical evaluative deliberation framed by the fundamental, comprehensive question, then it should be held to standards appropriate to that more sophisticated nature. That is, our conception of the proper or appropriate standards for practical reason should reflect its full nature: it should not be held merely to standards appropriate to a much more limited, parochial faculty. Just as we hold adults to higher standards than we do children, given the richer capacities possessed by adults, which carry with them higher legitimate expectations, in the same way, we should hold the robust form of practical reason we actually possess to higher standards than we would apply to more limited cognitive faculties. This is itself, of course, a *normative* claim, but it is a plausible one that should be amenable to those who, like ardent realists, accept that there are fundamental normative facts.[30]

How, then, should we think of the appropriate standards for our faculty of practical reason as we've described it? Given its capacity for comprehensive, critical evaluative deliberation, its *proper aim* or *target* is not merely something like desire-satisfaction as such: it is instead nothing less than *all-things-considered goodness of action, or acting well without qualification, in the overall circumstances one is in.* If practical reason is capable of framing its deliberations around that fundamental, comprehensive practical question, and assuming there are indeed correct answers to that question, then practical reason should be held to a standard that makes nothing less than success along those lines – that is, *deliberating soundly to action that constitutes acting well without qualification* – the proper target of its deliberative activity.

According to this neo-Aristotelian conception of practical reason, then, considerations have normative force in practical deliberation – providing *good reasons* for performing certain actions – not simply by helping to show that so acting would satisfy desires or promote interests, and so on, but *by helping to show that so acting would constitute acting well* (action that is, in the circumstances, all-things-considered good). On this model, that is how deliberations are appropriately settled, and so what makes certain considerations constitute genuine normative reasons for acting: their constituting genuine reasons is a function of how they bear on that fundamental, comprehensive, evaluative issue concerning action.

Returning, then, to the standards of action cited in claim 7, grounded in normative features of reality: Do these standards have genuine normative authority for us, as something we have good reason to care about and organize our lives around as rational agents? On the present picture of practical reason, they will have such authority just in case they bear relevantly on what we have

---

[30] Or at least this is so on the assumption that there is actually such a thing as all-things-considered goodness of action (or acting well without qualification) along with unqualified reasons or all-things-considered "oughts" of practical reason. Some theorists are skeptical of this (Copp 2007; Conee 2016), and if they're right in rejecting such things then it won't be true that practical reason is appropriately governed by standards that presuppose them. This would be problematic for ardent ethical realism, conceived as embracing a robust categorical ethical normativity.

identified as the proper concern of practical reason: all-things-considered good-ness of action, or acting well without qualification, in one's total circumstances. But this connection is indeed a very plausible one: for what better candidate for all-things-considered goodness of action than *action that is appropriately fitting to all the various objective evaluative or normative aspects of things one is encountering in one's circumstances* (such as the badness of the suffering of sentient beings, or the dignity of persons)? And that is precisely what the ethical standards in claim 7 would be prescribing: action that that is overall most fitting to those evaluative or normative features of reality, as encountered in various combinations and sets of circumstances.

This, then, is precisely the convergence we needed. The details will, of course, be complicated since what is overall most fitting may depend on complex interactions among different values that may stand in some tension. This is precisely what a virtue-theoretic account seeks to fill out in telling us, for example, how values bound up with beneficence and values bound up with justice interact when they conflict, as part of a specification of beneficence and justice (though there may be limits to the extent to which this is codifiable in anything like general principles). When does justice, in the name of respecting one person's rights, require forgoing the mitigation of another's suffering that would otherwise be called for by beneficence? When do the goals of benefi-cence instead override the usual requirements of justice? A developed account of ethical standards would need to illuminate such issues.

The present point is just that if there are indeed facts about the sort of action that would be prescribed by the standards in claim 7, then such action is naturally suited to fill the role of proper aim or concern of practical reason. And that means that those standards are precisely the ones that have genuine normative authority for us as the standards that appropriately guide our practical reasoning. Or at least this will be so on the assumption that we are capable, with education and ethical training, of grasping these standards and related facts about fitting action: for it would otherwise be hard to see how such standards could play this role with respect to our practical reason and have normative authority for us. Incorporating that epistemic assumption (for which the ardent realist will eventually have to provide some positive account), we therefore now have the connection we were looking for and the final claim of ardent ethical realism:

(8) **Knowable and Normatively Authoritative Standards**: The objectively fitting set of ethical standards in claim 7, favored by reality itself, is knowable by us, and it is normatively authoritative for us because the sort of action it prescribes is precisely the sort of action that is the proper concern or aim of practical reason.

With claims 7 and 8, we complete the characterization of ardent ethical realism, which holds that there is a set of ethical standards that (i) is objectively favored by reality itself by being grounded in irreducibly evaluative or normative aspects of reality, articulating what it is to live in a way that is inherently fitting to those features, and that (ii) is knowable and is normatively authoritative for us by virtue of prescribing action that is also the proper concern of practical reason itself. This is because the action that is *inherently fitting or appropriately responsive to all relevant values* one encounters is also the action that is *all-things-considered good* or constitutes *acting well without qualification*.

The way this last point is framed, in irreducibly normative terms about action that is appropriately responsive to all the values in play, is important. This is because it eliminates a persistent "open question" worry that plagues any attempt to capture normative authority that avoids irreducibly normative claims. For any standards that are recommended to us as underwritten by factors cashed out in nonnormative terms, such as those involving natural teleology or psychological or sociological theories, we can always wonder from the perspective of autonomous deliberation: Why should we care above all else about *that*? And it is hard to see how that normative gap can be filled in without just arising again. By contrast, there is no similar normative gap when it comes to standards underwritten simply by the *normative* fact that they articulate inherently fitting and appropriate responses to all relevant evaluative or normative aspects of reality. We might always reasonably wonder why we should care about standards derived from certain biological or psychological or sociological facts, for example; but there is no compelling analogous question: "sure, I grant that this set of standards articulates what is necessary in order to live in a way that involves inherently fitting responses to all the real and objective evaluative or normative features I encounter in the world (such as the goodness of happiness, the badness of suffering, or the dignity of persons), but why should I care about that?"

To ask that question would be to ask for a reason to care about all-things-considered goodness of one's action or acting well without qualification. But the view of practical reason laid out earlier closes off that question by presenting such goodness of action as the proper aim of practical reason itself, so that this is precisely what practical reasons are ultimately all *about*. Skeptics may of course doubt whether there really are such objective and irreducibly normative features of reality and resultant standards to begin with. But *if* there are, as ardent realists maintain, then this line of questions that keeps arising in connection with claims (like H and T) that avoid irreducibly normative appeals would not arise here, in connection with the standards cited in 7 and 8: the question would finally be closed (FitzPatrick 2018c).

3.4 Summary of the Characterization of Ethical Realism

We have characterized ethical realism using eight central claims, summarized just below. On the broadest construal of ethical realism, any view that accepts the first two claims counts as ethical realism. I argued that such a construal is too broad to be very useful. The most common understanding of ethical realism adds at least the third claim, and given recent developments among "quietist" nonnaturalists there is also good reason to add the fourth claim for a properly realist view (though there may be gray areas). Given current terminological practices, it makes sense to count any view that accepts the first four claims as a form of ethical realism.

I have also argued, however, that being genuinely realist *about ethics* probably involves more than that. I therefore introduced four additional claims, 5–8, which, when added to the others, give us what I've called "ardent ethical realism," a view that arguably has the best claim to be a paradigm of ethical realism. There are, of course, other ways in which these latter claims might be formulated, which still capture the crucial ideas. What we've described here is thus intended to be at least a good representative of a group of similar views that might be regarded as fully realist about ethics. Here is the complete set of claims:

(1) **Representational Content**: Ethical sentences express propositions that can be straightforwardly true or false by virtue of their representational ethical content; ethical sentences and propositions are *truth-apt* due to their representational content, and ethical claims purport to state ethical facts. Likewise, ethical judgments are *cognitive* states with the same representational ethical content. Ethical claims express such beliefs, which can likewise be straightforwardly true or false.

(2) **Truth**: At least some positive ethical sentences, and the propositions expressed by them, are in fact *true*, and straightforwardly so, in the way ordinary descriptive sentences or propositions are: they are true because the world is in fact as it is represented to be by the propositional content in question. There are thus genuine *ethical properties and facts*, by virtue of which some of our positive ethical claims succeed in being straightforwardly *true* when they accurately represent a state of affairs involving the instantiation of ethical properties.

(3) **Stance-Independence**: There are positive "[ethical] truths that obtain independently of any preferred perspective in the sense that *the [ethical] standards that fix the [particular ethical] facts are not made true or correct by virtue of their ratification from within any given actual or hypothetical*

perspective," such as one employing idealizing conditions or procedures (Shafer-Landau 2003, 15).

(4) **Ontological Commitment**: Basic ethical truths, which are constitutive of the true or correct set of ethical standards that (together with circumstantial facts) fix particular ethical facts, have truth-makers within the ontology of the world/reality (in the form of worldly ethical properties and facts).

(5) **Favoring by Reality Itself**: Among the objective features of the world or reality are some that make it the case that "reality itself favors certain ways of valuing and acting" over others (Eklund 2017, 1), such that a certain set of ethical standards is in fact the objectively appropriate or proper one for ethically evaluating and governing human practical life.

(6) **Irreducibly Normative Reality**: There are at least some *irreducibly normative properties and facts*, which (given claims 4 and 5) are *worldly* (part of reality) and so *ontologically* robust, and either fundamental or grounded partly in more fundamental normative properties and facts, such that there is normative reality "all the way down."

(7) **Objectively Fitting Standards**: There are features of reality with an irreducibly normative nature that consists partly in making certain responses to those features *inherently fitting* or *unfitting*. Such features may thus be understood to ground a certain set of standards for feeling, choice, and action as the set that is *aligned with normative reality*, by virtue of articulating *inherently fitting responses* to these features as they are encountered (in various circumstances and combinations) in practical life.

(8) **Knowable and Normatively Authoritative Standards**: The objectively fitting set of ethical standards in claim 7, favored by reality itself, is knowable by us, and it is normatively authoritative for us because the sort of action it prescribes is precisely the sort of action that is the proper concern or aim of practical reason.

It is worth making explicit an important qualification regarding this endorsement of objectively fitting and authoritative ethical standards. Ardent ethical realists are concerned to defend the objectivity and categorical normative force of at least a core of ethics, consisting in certain basic and universal ethical values and standards, such as human dignity and the basic standards it plausibly grounds across cultures and times (*contra* ethical relativism). Endorsing such an objective set of ethical parameters, however, doesn't mean that they come anywhere close to prescribing all the details of what a well-lived human life looks like. For one thing, many aspects of human life, at both cultural and individual levels, are simply irrelevant to these objective ethical values: they are just a matter of ethically irrelevant variation in sensibilities, customs, tastes, and so on (even though they might sometimes mistakenly have been thought to be real ethical issues). Ethical realism does not commit one to thinking that it is the role of objective ethical values to micromanage every detail of our lives.

Moreover, even where objective values are in play, there will often be a number of equally good ways of respecting them, at both cultural and individual levels. There may be many *equally fitting* responses to the values in question. This is a familiar and plausible kind of ethical *pluralism* (not to be confused with blanket relativism), grounded in a recognition that differences in natural and cultural circumstances can sometimes make a difference to what it is right or wrong to do or what specific obligations people may have. For example, even if we think that it is part of the correct set of ethical standards that people have some ethical obligation to care for elderly family members, that obligation may take different specific forms depending on conventions of familial organization and care. So even universal standards at a general level may take on contextual variations at a more detailed level of description. Ardent ethical realism does not deny that.

Similarly, there may well be cases where there is no determinate resolution to a conflict that arises among competing values. In such hard cases, not only might equally wise people disagree on what to do but there may be no fact of the matter about the correct resolution. Ardent ethical realism insists only that there is enough of an objective basis for ethics in worldly values to settle at least an important core set of moral questions. Exactly how far that goes can be left open for further exploration, just as with questions about how far pluralism might extend for various issues.

4 Support and Challenges

I have sought to bring out some of the motivations and challenges for ethical realism in the course of developing it. We turn now to these issues more explicitly.

4.1 An Argument for Ethical Realism?

It might be thought that proponents of ethical realism should be able to provide some overarching argument for it, as one might offer an argument for dualism or for the absence of free will. As should be clear by now, however, this would be a misguided expectation. Given the wide range of views that fall under the umbrella of ethical realism, arguments for ethical realism will be as diverse as the theoretical concerns emphasized by those views. There will be some commonalities, insofar as any argument for some form of realism will have to make a case for a semantics of ethical discourse that satisfies the first two claims in ways that also conform to claims 3 and 4 – thus avoiding expressivism, error theory, constructivism, and so on. But the details will vary greatly, and this will be reflected in the argumentative support appropriate to different views.

A naturalist committed only to the first four claims, for example, might appeal to functional or explanatory roles associated with ethical concepts to explain how reference is fixed for them and how their referents thus turn out to be (or be constituted by) the natural properties that fill those roles. This could be modeled on a functional role view of a concept such as redness, where the reference is fixed by a role associated *a priori* with the concept of redness, such as that of causing things to look red to normal perceivers under standard conditions; then the idea is that whatever microphysical property of objects plays that role (which is an *a posteriori* matter) is the referent of the concept of redness – the property we were in fact talking about all along when speaking of redness (Smith 2004, 197). In the same way, a realist functional role view might claim, for example, that as an a priori matter "rightness" refers to whatever natural property fills the objective role of promoting social stability so that whichever natural property turns out (a posteriori) to make actions promote social stability will be the property of rightness we've been talking about all along in ethical discourse. This would be to argue for a naturalistic version of ethical realism employing an attractive theory of reference from other domains and using causal-explanatory roles to establish the ontological credentials of the properties identified as ethical ones.[31]

Such an argumentative strategy, however, would be a nonstarter for ardent realists, for whom establishing a reference to such natural properties would not advance the case for *ethical truth* as they understand it (see Section 2.2). They will need a very different sort of argument for ardent ethical realism, involving a different picture of what ethical discourse is ultimately *about*, what ethical properties and facts would have to be like, and what the world would have to be like to accommodate them – as set forth in claims 5–8. So there is nothing like a single, overarching "argument for ethical realism" that would cover such radically different views. Instead, there will be various kinds of support for different versions of ethical realism, depending on which of the eight claims they accept and how they fill them out.

Again, there will be some commonalities. All realists will argue, against expressivists, that ethical discourse has representational content, and there will be overlap in their negative arguments. The two very different realists above will both emphasize that ethical expressions and sentences behave

---

[31] Michael Smith (2004) discusses and rejects the above sort of realist or "externalist" functional role view, associated with "Cornell Realism," though he embraces an "internalist" form of functional role view (which would not count as realist under our characterization, given its stance-dependence). For criticism of both forms of naturalistic functional role view, see FitzPatrick (2014a).

grammatically and logically just like descriptive expressions and sentences: we can formulate questions using ethical expressions, negate ethical sentences, or embed them within conditionals, where they will enter into inferential relations just as ordinary descriptive sentences do (the "Frege-Geach Problem"). For example, using ordinary principles of logic, we can infer from

(i) If it's wrong to lie, then it's wrong to use social media to spread others' lies, and

(ii) It's wrong to lie,

the conclusion that

(iii) It's wrong to use social media to spread others' lies.

Expressivists, of course, have offered sophisticated proposals to account for such things in nonrepresentational terms.[32] But both realists above might join forces in arguing that such attempts at an expressivist semantics of moral discourse fall short in various ways, favoring a representationalist account. Error theorists may join in the effort as well.

After that, however, the strategies diverge sharply. The error theorist departs from the two realists, arguing that the contents represented in ethical claims are all false. But the two realists quickly part ways as well. The semantic account offered by the naturalist realist above might save some notion of "ethical truth," but only in a way that both the ardent realist and the error theorist will regard as tantamount to changing the subject, capturing truths stripped of the objective prescriptivity that made the idea of ethical truth interesting in the first place. The ardent realist will instead turn to very different kinds of properties and truths in defending realist claims. We will focus in what follows on the kind of support that might be given for ardent ethical realism, and then turn to some challenges it faces.

4.2 Supporting Ardent Ethical Realism

Given the nature of ardent ethical realism, it should come as no surprise if the kind of support appropriate to it differs from that for other metaethical views. In particular, it should not be assumed that there should be any viable way of arguing for ardent ethical realism by starting from ethically neutral premises about the semantics of ethical language based on empirical observation of how we use words and concepts, or about causal-explanatory roles played by certain natural properties, and so on.[33] To understand the argumentative support

---

[32] See, e.g., Blackburn (1984, 1993) and Gibbard (1990).

[33] The critique in Horgan and Timmons (1991) of such argumentative approaches constitutes substantial common ground with ardent ethical realism, despite the divergence from realism in their positive account.

relevant to ardent realism we need to look at what actually drives proponents to embrace it.

Ardent ethical realism is a metaethical view that is arrived at primarily by:

(1) Starting from the perspective of an engaged and committed ethical agent;
(2) Reflecting on that first-order ethical experience and finding it compelling in certain respects as it stands, without deflation, which thus guides metaethical inquiry going forward;
(3) Formulating ardent ethical realism as a working hypothesis to account for that ethical experience taken at face value;
(4) Considering rival metaethical views in light of how well they capture and cohere with that ethical experience, without deflation;
(5) Ruling out views that either fail to do so or independently seem philosophically less tenable than ardent realism;
(6) Defending ardent realism against various objections; and
(7) Finding that on balance ardent realism seems more attractive all-things-considered than rival metaethical views.

This is nothing like an argument drawing on scientific data or importing ethically neutral principles of semantics or metaphysics into the ethical domain to establish a metaethical view. It is instead a philosophical progression from reflection on engaged ethical experience to a metaethical view that seems necessary for making adequate sense of it. As such, it is – unlike most metaethical arguments – not the sort of argumentative path that could in principle be taken by an amoral anthropologist with philosophical training in semantics, metaphysics, and epistemology. It begins essentially in engaged ethical experience.

Now we all know that experience can be misleading, which raises the possibility that we might be led astray by this methodology, beginning with first-order ethical experience taken at face value and allowing this to shape our metaethics. Perhaps, as the error theorist thinks, the ethical appearances that drive some of us to ardent realism are misleading. Others will worry that the proposed methodology sounds like an argument by elimination, which is a tall order in such complex theoretical territory. Doesn't this, then, place the ardent realist on awfully shaky ground? Wouldn't it be *safer* instead to adopt a methodology that doesn't give such weight to our experience as ethically engaged agents, but instead just imports general principles from semantics, metaphysics and epistemology (along with scientific data) and applies them to the ethical domain, thus telling us how we really should be interpreting our ethical experience? I believe the answer to both questions is "no."

First, it is important not to misunderstand the proposed theoretical reliance on ethical experience. It is not that we should cavalierly (and implausibly) assume that all of our ethical beliefs are correct, or that our initial interpretation of our ethical experience is immune to being overturned by further metaethical inquiry. We should expect that we harbor some false ethical beliefs or that some ethical appearances will turn out to be inaccurate; and obviously in the context of first-order ethical debate it would be question-begging just to assume that an ethical belief at issue is correct. The point is just that in doing *metaethics*, we can reasonably treat at least some core aspects of our most central and settled experience as engaged ethical agents – that is, certain core ethical appearances – as guiding and at least defeasibly constraining our metaethical theorizing.[34]

We thus begin by considering central and stable ethical beliefs reflecting core values, such as:

> E: It is wrong to discriminate against people, in distributing educational and employment opportunities, based on their race, gender or sexual orientation or identity.

Then we reflect on our experience of this ethical commitment: Does this appear to be something that is simply open to cultural or individual choice – a stance to be embraced or not, without objective error either way – or does it instead appear to be something to which we are committed because it is true? And if the latter, what sort of truth does this seem to be, and what kind of practical claim does it make on us?

For at least many of us who take E seriously, our experience of it is as of something both *true* and *important*, such that its truth:

  (i) is *objective* (independent of our culture's – or our own individual – choices or desires or attitudes or laws or current practices, etc.),
 (ii) is relevant to *unqualified evaluation of human action and character*, and
(iii) *bears authoritatively on how we should live* (i.e., it cannot without error be shrugged off).

These are the kinds of core aspects of our ethical experience that we bring to the metaethical table as starting points to guide our theorizing. We then seek a semantics, metaphysics, and epistemology of the ethical domain that *captures and coheres with* this experience, without denying, deflating, or distorting it. This does not mean denying that some other metaethical picture could turn out to be correct – even one, such as error theory, that rejects the veridicality of this experience; nor does it mean denying that any metaethical argument could ever

---

[34] This might be framed as an application of the *principle of phenomenal conservativism* to metaethical inquiry (Huemer 2005).

dislodge this commitment to a metaethical picture that captures these ethical appearances. Ardent realism doesn't preclude intellectual humility about difficult philosophical matters.

The point is just that we approach metaethics from a starting point that finds certain appearances from our core ethical experience sufficiently compelling that we see our project, in the first instance, as one of seeking a metaethical interpretation of that experience that adequately captures and coheres with the ethical appearances presented in that experience. This can change if, in the course of inquiry, we come across contravening metaethical considerations so compelling that we find ourselves more convinced by them than we are by the appearances bound up with our deepest ethical experience. In that case, we will be led away from the attempt to vindicate those appearances and accept some deflationary metaethics. But if, after careful philosophical examination, we continue to find an interpretation of our ethical experience along the lines of that suggested for E more compelling than any contravening considerations intended to "debunk" or deflate it (such as the error theorist's "argument from queerness" or evolutionary debunkers' arguments against realism), then we will continue to shape our metaethics as needed to accommodate the ethical appearances as they stand. And this is how some of us are led to ardent ethical realism, at least when it seems to do the job better than alternative views and survives challenges without unacceptable costs.[35]

This argumentative approach has obvious limitations. For one thing, it doesn't even pretend to offer an ethically neutral Archimedean point from which to demonstrate to all parties the truth of ardent realism. It will not get traction against an amoralist or nihilist, or against someone (such as a subjectivist or relativist) who just feels little or no intuitive pull toward the claims made about E earlier (though nothing prevents the ardent realist from engaging in other arguments to try to dislodge particular skeptical claims as they arise). The ardent realist should thus acknowledge that the argumentative posture of this approach is more defense-oriented than offense-oriented: it is not designed to show all opponents that they must accept the view, but instead aims to provide reasonable justification for maintaining this metaethical position given certain starting points that at least many find compelling.

Whether these limitations are a strike against the view depends on how one sees the point of philosophical argumentation. Some may think that a good philosophical argument ought to be able to convince any rational subject of the

---

[35] In answering an important challenge to realists issued by Horgan and Timmons (2008, 2018), I make the case (in FitzPatrick 2021) that if we take the moral phenomenology seriously, then we will in fact be led in the direction of an ontologically committed ethical realism (and away from alternatives such as their cognitivist expressivism or Kantian rationalism, for example).

truth of its conclusion. Arguments are often presented in that light – with surprisingly little reflection, it seems, on how rarely philosophers on opposite sides of any interesting debate actually wind up convincing each other with such an argument. It may actually be more realistic instead to view the process more in terms of providing defeasible justification, for those who accept certain starting points, to provisionally adopt a theory on the grounds that it best coheres with them. This requires giving up certain argumentative ambitions, but it also allows us to reject any demand to set aside our experiential starting points and proceed without them, following metaethical inquiry wherever it then leads. Others may do that if they like, championing ideals like theoretical parsimony even if this results in a deflationary interpretation of our ethical experience. But this can hardly be demanded of those who find the experiential starting points more compelling than any such theoretical ideals. Any methodological approach that so discounts those ethical appearances will seem like the *opposite* of the "safe" path to us.

The adoption of the more modest conception of argumentative support also speaks to the worry about arguing by elimination. Such a strategy is indeed problematic if one is seeking a knockdown argument for some view, but it needn't disturb us on the proposed model. We should just acknowledge that the process of eliminating competing views is open-ended, lending provisional support to ardent realism that is only as strong as the cases made against competing views and always open to challenge by a new competitor. Ardent realists will just have to devote ongoing attention to showing that competing metaethical views – such as "less ardent" versions of realism, or neo-Kantian constructivism, or quasi-realist expressivism – do not ultimately do as good as job at capturing our core ethical experience without deflation. That is what much of the argumentative support for ardent realism will look like.

We have already examined what ardent realists find missing in certain forms of naturalist realism, which is what drives them to claims 5–8 about the kinds of properties and relations the world contains. This amounts to argumentative support for being an ardent realist if one is going to be a realist at all and accepts certain starting points: we seem to need to go all the way to ardent realism to make full sense of the ethical appearances. But what about the possibility of capturing the trappings of ardent realism within a *non*realist metaethical framework? Can that be done in a way that equally captures and coheres with our ethical experience, without deflation, while avoiding metaphysical commitments to irreducibly ethical properties and facts? If so, ardent realism might seem extravagant: Why posit such a richly value-laden world if we can get everything we want without it? So ardent realists need to try to rule out such competitors.

Three prominent approaches that purport to make ardent realism unnecessary in this way are neo-Kantian constitutivism, other (non-constitutivist) forms of ethical constructivism, and quasi-realist expressivism. Kant himself famously sought to derive a rich, categorically authoritative, or rationally binding morality simply from principles of pure practical reason. Descendants of this approach often explicitly deny any sort of realist value inherent in the world (even in rational beings) while still purporting to derive categorically binding principles from basic conditions of agency. This includes a principle committing us to valuing persons *as if* they had the sort of inherent worth and dignity a realist might attribute to them (Korsgaard 1996, 2003, 2009). But then who needs real value in the world if, for all practical purposes, we are *already* subject to the same categorically binding moral standards just by being agents?

Other constructivists instead seek to derive facts about value, obligation, or reasons for acting from contingent elements of human psychology, such as desires or attitudes, as filtered through certain hypothetical idealizing procedures that can be specified in an ethically neutral way, involving enhanced empirical information, deliberative procedures, and so on. And again, if ethical facts can all be captured in this way then it will seem unnecessary to posit irreducibly evaluative or normative facts in the world.

Finally, quasi-realist expressivists have a different way of making ardent realism seem unnecessary. They argue that whatever ardent realists want to say about moral requirements – about how they are objective and normatively binding on everyone – can be captured, without deflation, in terms of the contents of the commitments or attitudes or plans we *express* with such claims. Everything the ardent realist wants to say can be echoed by the expressivist, the difference being that the latter will give an expressivist account of what is happening in making such claims, which needn't appeal to real ethical properties in the world (Gibbard 1990, 2003, 2010; Blackburn 1993; Horgan and Timmons 2006).

A major part of why I remain an ardent realist is that I am not persuaded that such approaches succeed in delivering the goods as advertised. Neo-Kantian constitutivism promises rich, normatively authoritative principles capturing all of morality without relying on any substantive evaluative or normative posits about the world, deriving all of this just from conditions for agency. Naturally, it would require powerful arguments to accomplish such an ambitious derivation, and if those arguments seemed promising then those of us pursuing the methodology described earlier might embrace this metaphysically more parsimonious project. The reason I have not done so is that I do not believe such neo-Kantian constitutivist arguments succeed or show promise of being reparable in ways that would make them successful. So an important part of my own argumentative support for ardent realism has involved detailed attempts to show that we cannot get the rich results in question in the ways proposed by such neo-Kantian accounts, thus provisionally narrowing down relevant alternatives.[36]

We may also have reasons to doubt the adequacy of other forms of constructivism, stemming mainly from skepticism that the full range of facts about value, obligation, and categorical reasons can be captured through any scheme seeking to derive them from contingent facts about human psychology (FitzPatrick 2004, 2008, 2014a). For example, even where these psychological factors are hypothetically subjected to idealizing conditions such as deliberation in light of full empirical information, very different psychological starting points are likely to lead to significantly different outcomes involving motivation or judgment. So views that make ethical facts functions of such outcomes may not seem likely to capture the kinds of universal and categorical facts ardent realists are after. More generally, ardent realists will resist holding ethical facts hostage to what can be derived from contingent facts about human psychology through ethically neutral idealizing procedures. Part of the intuition behind ardent realism is the sense that ethical facts are not contingent on and derivative from psychological facts in this way, but are a fundamental and irreducible aspect of the world in their own right.

In the case of quasi-realist expressivism, the question is whether such a view really succeeds in capturing the ethical appearances without objectionable deflation. In one sense, it may seem that it does: for whatever content ardent realists offer in laying out their rich understanding of ethical reality, in terms of objectivity, independence and normative authority, the expressivist can echo in full, without watering it down (see Section 1.1). The problem, however, is that in going on to give a metaethical construal of all this talk merely in terms of commitments or attitudes or plans, the expressivist seems to be engaging in a deeper sort of deflation after all. In fact, there is a kind of *parity problem* introduced here that parallels the one we saw earlier with certain naturalist forms of realism.

To see this, suppose I say that tormenting animals for fun is wrong, and that this is true independently of what we or anyone else thinks or feels about it. On an expressivist view, in saying this, I am expressing certain attitudes or commitments or plans, not representing the world as being a certain way ethically. And an expressivist who shares my attitudes can say exactly the same thing I say, expressing all the same attitudes and thus sounding as realist as I do. But now what are we to say about a third party who says the opposite – that

---

[36] The details of both the neo-Kantian constitutivist arguments and the critiques of them are too complex to summarize here, but interested readers can find discussion in FitzPatrick (2005, 2013).

tormenting animals for fun is *just fine*, and that *this* is true independently of what we or anyone else thinks about it? Well, the expressivist who shares my attitude can further express this attitude by saying that this other person's claim is false, and it's false independently of what anyone happens to think about it: tormenting animals for fun is *not* fine, and so on. And again, that may sound a lot like what the realist wants to say. But notice that this other person, with the contrary attitude, can again express *their* attitude by now saying exactly parallel things about *us* and our claims, saying that *we're* objectively mistaken. And the problem now is that there do not seem to be any resources within a purely expressivist picture to give sense to the idea that one party is in fact nontrivially *correct* about this while the other is *mistaken*. Both sides seem to be exactly on a par objectively speaking.

Trivially, of course, we can again express our attitudes by saying that *we* are correct and the other person is mistaken; but the other person can go on to do exactly the same in the opposite direction. Without something to *break the symmetry* here, we have not been able even to give a sense to the ardent realist's idea of objective, nonrelative ethical truth or correctness. And that is precisely why the ardent realist posits worldly ethical properties and facts: to break the above symmetry. Regardless of what we may or may not be able to *prove* to someone else's satisfaction (which is a different issue), there is at least a clear sense, on the ardent realist's picture, of what it would *be*, objectively and nontrivially, for one in fact to be correct while the other is mistaken, in terms of *fit or lack of fit with real, worldly values* such as the intrinsic badness of suffering. All of this strongly suggests, then, that quasi-realist expressivism does not give us everything the ardent realist desires. It may allow one to say realist-sounding things when expressing first-order ethical attitudes, but as a metaethical account it does not deliver the kind of objective ethical truth we were after.[37]

These examples are just meant to illustrate the argumentative progression toward ardent realism: if we maintain the theoretical goal of capturing a robust objectivity and categorical normative authority in ethics, and we find that alternative metaethical views seem not to succeed in this, then that provides justification for at least provisionally endorsing ardent ethical realism. This, I believe, is what argumentation in favor of ardent ethical realism properly looks like, and it will be an ongoing and open-ended project, engaging critically with

---

[37] Thus, as I argue in FitzPatrick (2011), while expressivists may sidestep a certain kind of charge of *relativism* (Horgan and Timmons 2006; Gibbard 2010), their arguments do not remove the deeper *parity* worry, as I've described it. Enoch (2010a) offers a related criticism in terms of a problematic *dependence* relation.

a wide variety of metaethical positions rather than some neat and static positive argument.

4.3 Challenges for Ardent Ethical Realism

There are a variety of challenges confronting ardent ethical realism. We have already noted one in connection with the categorical and unqualified normative authority of ethical requirements: to make sense of that idea we relied on the notion of unqualified reasons for acting or all-things-considered "oughts" of practical reason, properly guiding deliberation; and we needed to argue that this "ought" tracks *the same thing* tracked by the correct ethical standards: namely, unqualified, all-things-considered goodness of action. But it is not obvious that there is any such thing as unqualified, all-things-considered "oughts" of practical reason or goodness of action. Actions can be ethically or prudentially or aesthetically good, and there can be ethical or prudential or aesthetic reasons to do things. But is there also such a thing as action that is *unqualifiedly good all-things-considered*, or reasons that are not specific to a particular framework but are simply *unqualified reasons of concern to practical reason as such*, which it can use to adjudicate among competing reasons of particular kinds (e.g., prudential vs. ethical) to yield an unqualified and authoritative "ought"?

If not, as some claim (Copp 2007; Conee 2016), then an important part of the ardent realist's ambition would be misguided. So one important challenge will be to defend such ideas of unqualified and all-things-considered goodness and reasons, or something relevantly similar to them, against such challenges. In this final section, we will highlight some further challenges involving metaphysical and epistemic issues, and consider some directions realists might take in responding to them.

4.3.1 Metaphysical Worries

The most common metaphysical complaint against ardent ethical realism is also arguably the least compelling. Because ardent realism posits properties and facts that would typically be regarded as "nonnatural" (Section 3.2), it is often accused of being metaphysically extravagant or indulging in a "spooky" metaphysics. As we have seen, however, the "nonnaturalism" of the properties and facts posited by ardent realism amounts to nothing more than their having an irreducibly evaluative or normative nature. There is nothing inherently obscure in this idea. It can be illustrated with such plausible claims as that pointless suffering is intrinsically bad, making it inherently unfitting to be indifferent to it – with the added claim that this fact is basic in the sense that it cannot even in principle be reduced to (or accounted for by appeal to) anything fully articulable in nonnormative terms (coming from biology, psychology, sociology, etc.).

Such claims might turn out to be false, but it is unclear why one should find anything outrageous in the idea that the world contains such properties and facts. A common form of scientism encourages the feeling that anything not scientifically detectable and explicable is thereby ontologically suspicious, but this is little more than a metaphysical prejudice, and merely labeling things like irreducibly normative properties "spooky" is not an argument against them. Sometimes it's objected that such properties would be *unlike any others* in the world. But it's hard to see why that should be thought to count against them: one should not *expect* them to be like other properties that are not irreducibly normative, such as shape or mass, any more than one would expect irreducibly phenomenal properties to be like non-phenomenal properties. Even in physics, it is no objection to dark energy, for example, that it is not like other forms of energy. The world may simply contain a variety of diverse phenomena with different natures, in which case it is misguided to object to an otherwise plausible posit simply on the grounds that such a thing would be very different from *other* things.

It's true that we take on metaphysical commitments by positing irreducibly normative properties and facts, and perhaps that is a kind of "theoretical cost": all else being equal we should favor theories with fewer such commitments. But the ardent realist's claim is precisely that all else is *not* equal here: dispensing with such properties and facts appears to undermine our ability to properly capture relevant aspects of ethical experience – at least if the ardent realist's interpretation of that experience and their claims about the inadequacies of alternative metaethical frameworks are correct. So while ardent realism is less parsimonious than other views, it's unclear that its proponents need to be worried about that.

A more interesting metaphysical challenge involves the relation of *supervenience*. It is a widely held principle that whatever exactly the relation is between ethical and natural properties, it is intimate enough that two things cannot differ in their ethical properties unless there is some difference in their underlying natural properties; it cannot be the case, for example, that two actions are indiscernible with respect to their natural features and yet one is right while the other is wrong – as if ethical properties could float freely and independently above ordinary natural properties. But this constraint might seem hard to explain if ethical properties are *nonnaturalistic*: For in that case, what ties them to natural properties, making them supervene in this way?

This can at least partly be answered straightforwardly using the standard-based model we've discussed. In this model, ethical properties are *resultant*

properties that are instantiated when a thing has certain familiar natural properties (the resultance-base properties) that make it meet or violate relevant ethical
standards. The nonnaturalism comes into this picture only insofar as we posit
irreducibly normative aspects of the world – such as the badness of suffering or
the dignity of persons – as grounding the ethical standards (assuming that
irreducibly normative properties count as "nonnatural"). Ethical rightness,
then, is nonnaturalistic in the sense that it cannot be fully explicated by appeal
to natural properties and facts, but requires an appeal to irreducibly normative
ones underlying the standards that figure constitutively into ethical properties.
But this does not in the least imply that rightness is some otherworldly property
that could float freely from natural properties.

Since rightness is a resultant property, it is intimately connected to the natural
resultance-base properties, being *partly a function* of those properties (cf.
Dancy 1993, 79). On this model, given a certain set of ethical standards, no
two actions could have all the same natural resultance-base properties and yet
differ in their ethical properties. Such a thing would require that the same set of
resultance-base properties is such that it both makes something overall satisfy
the standards and makes something overall violate the standards, which is
incoherent. We can thus explain ordinary supervenience on the standard-
based model, at least assuming a single set of standards, even though they are
nonnaturalistic (FitzPatrick 2008).

A deeper challenge remains, however. There is still the matter of explaining
supervenience at the fundamental level and across possible worlds. The ardent
realist holds that some familiar elements of the world have irreducibly normative features that ground a single set of correct ethical standards, and this is
meant to apply across possible worlds: if suffering in the actual world has an
intrinsic badness that partly grounds ethical standards forbidding cruelty, then it
does so in other possible worlds too, and similarly with rational nature and
dignity, resulting (plausibly) in basic ethical standards that are *invariant* across
possible worlds. But how is this to be explained? Why do these underlying,
irreducibly normative features attach to these elements of natural reality in just
these ways and of necessity? Here we seem to be positing a necessary connection between two very different kinds of things – natural entities and irreducibly
normative aspects of them – that seems just to be *brute*. And the positing of such
brute connections among distinct entities in the world may seem metaphysically
suspect, violating "Hume's dictum" against such things and imposing
a significant cost on such a theory (McPherson 2012).

It is hard to know how to assess this worry. It would certainly be theoretically
embarrassing to have nothing to say to explain the higher-level supervenience
discussed earlier, such as why two naturalistically indiscernible actions or

agents cannot differ in their moral status: an appeal to brute connections to explain every such case would be desperate and plainly unsatisfactory. But we've seen that the ardent realist has a straightforward explanation for that familiar sort of supervenience. The only place brute connections are coming in is at the most *fundamental* level: between the grounds of the ethical standards and the natural elements of the world that those grounds are associated with, as irreducibly normative aspects of them. So is it implausible that the world should feature such brute connections?

Some metaphysicians may find it so, and the appearance of oddness will be at its strongest when considering the matter purely in the abstract: For why should nature produce such inexplicable necessary connections between such different things (McPherson 2012)? But the sense of mystery and oddness fades quickly when we consider actual examples. I have proposed a dual-aspect theory (FitzPatrick 2008) according to which some elements of the world, such as suffering, have in addition to their various empirical aspects some irreducibly evaluative aspects as well, such as reason-giving intrinsic badness that makes certain responses to suffering inherently fitting and others unfitting. This is posited as a necessary, brute connection between *suffering* and *reason-giving intrinsic badness*, the latter being a necessary aspect of the former – part of its *essential nature*. Now in reflecting on our ethically laden experience of suffering (both our own and that of others), does it seem bizarre or mysterious that suffering should have, as part of its essential nature, this sort of normative aspect to it, such that certain responses to it are inherently fitting and others are inherently unfitting?[38]

Speaking for myself, this doesn't seem bizarre at all: it seems as intuitively plausible as things get in ethics. Instead of denying it because it violates some independent metaphysical scruple against brute necessary connections in the world, I take this example as evidence against such metaphysical prohibitions. In line with the ardent realist methodology outlined earlier, we might reasonably allow our reflective ethical experience to shape our metaphysics rather than forcing our interpretation of our ethical experience into a box constrained by

---

[38] Stephanie Leary (2017) argues that non-naturalists can appeal to an essentialist metaphysics to provide a metaphysical explanation for the supervenience of the normative on the natural, while avoiding reliance on the sort of brute necessary connections to which McPherson objects. As indicated in the text, I am sympathetic to the metaphysical appeal to essences, but I do not believe that this essentialist non-naturalism avoids positing brute necessary connections: it still does so within the specification of relevant essences themselves. For example, in my terms we still have the necessary connection between the empirical and normative aspects of suffering; in Leary's framework we still have the necessary connection between *being a painful experience* and *being bad* in the conditional proposition that *if x is a painful experience then x is bad*, which is partly constitutive of the essence of the "hybrid property" *being in pain*. My point in the text is just that such connections needn't be thought strange.

independent metaphysical principles. If the ardent realist framework turns out to be the best way to make sense of our ethical experience, and that requires positing such basic necessary connections, then our metaethics may wind up broadening our metaphysics.

4.3.2 Epistemological Worries

Ardent realism also faces epistemological challenges. We will discuss just two here – the problem of ethical disagreement and the theoretical demand to provide a positive account of how we come to have ethical knowledge.[39]

(i) The Problem of Ethical Disagreement

One puzzle for ardent realism is why, if there are objective and knowable ethical truths, there is persistent *ethical disagreement* (Mackie 1977). Some of the most familiar disagreement here is about notoriously controversial issues such as abortion or euthanasia, where even people who share basic ethical beliefs often diverge. But there is also deeper disagreement over core values or principles, as between advocates of universal human rights or moral equality among persons, and those who reject such views and hold incompatible beliefs. The existence of so much ethical disagreement might seem like strong evidence against the existence of objective and knowable ethical truths.

This worry is predicated on the assumption that if such truths existed then for the most part people would have grasped them and thus come to a far greater convergence of ethical belief. It is far from clear, however, that this assumption is true, and the ardent realist's reply will thus be to provide an account of why the level of disagreement we find is actually unsurprising even on a realist model. That is, we can explain why people often come to hold different beliefs even in the face of objective ethical truth. There are a number of points to make in this connection.

First, disagreements over notoriously hard cases are to be expected even if there are objective facts of the matter: cases like abortion count as hard cases precisely because there tend to be significant ethical considerations pulling in both directions and the proper resolution may turn on complex details in the

---

[39] I will here set aside the widely discussed "evolutionary debunking" challenge to ethical realism, which appeals to Darwinian considerations to "debunk" it, either by supporting ethical skepticism or by showing that realism would saddle us with an implausible ethical skepticism (Joyce 2006 and Street 2006, respectively). While such debunking arguments highlight possibilities that need to be taken seriously, and provide some considerations that indirectly raise challenges for certain forms of realism (discussed below), I have argued elsewhere that they overreach in their *debunking* aspirations and can be adequately defused even without having in hand a developed positive epistemic account for ethical realism (FitzPatrick 2014b, 2014c, and see also Shafer-Landau 2012).

circumstances or difficult issues such as how to determine an entity's moral status.

Second, as noted earlier, even the ardent realist will allow for a certain degree of pluralism such that in some such cases, especially where the balance of competing considerations is very close, there may not be a single correct answer, allowing for equally reasonable and virtuous people to come to different conclusions that are equally legitimate; such cases, involving a plurality of legitimate responses, are compatible with the existence of more general ethical truths that also rule out other responses as objectively mistaken.

A third point is that a great deal of ethical disagreement is due not to disagreement over basic values or principles but to differences in nonethical beliefs that bear on ethical issues. Disagreement over the ethics of continuing mass burning of fossil fuels, for example, is at least partly attributable not to basic differences in values but to widespread ignorance of its harmful effects on the climate: those who harbor such ignorance of relevant background facts will fail to draw the ethical conclusion that such activity is wrong, leading to ethical disagreement with those who are better informed. Such disagreement, however, casts no doubt on the existence of the ethical facts in question – either of the general underlying values (which again may be largely shared here) or of the more particular ethical facts. And a great deal of ethical disagreement likely falls into this category, such that it would be eliminated with improvements in factual knowledge about the world.

The example just given leads to a fourth point: even with regard to ordinary empirical matters – such as whether anthropogenic climate change is occurring, or whether certain vaccines are effective against a virus in a pandemic, or whether an election was stolen from a politician through a vast series of conspiracies – we find a striking amount of disagreement, yet we do not take this to cast doubt on the existence of objective truth about such things. Clearly, there are objective facts of the matter about each of these things, despite widespread disagreement about them. The disagreement doesn't make us doubt the existence of objective truth here because we have good explanations for why there is such disagreement despite the existence of objective facts – that is, disagreement due to various contributors to ignorance.

Recent years have made clear the effects of widespread misinformation and deliberate campaigns of disinformation by people with vested interests in managing others' beliefs to their advantage. Of particular relevance here is the social tendency to form tribalistic identities and loyalties that calcify related networks of beliefs, making them much less responsive to evidence and rational argumentation. Ethical beliefs are no less caught up in this web of epistemic distortion than empirical beliefs are – both derivatively, due to their dependence on certain empirical beliefs, and more fundamentally, as tribalistic identity and loyalty can greatly influence people's evaluative outlooks regardless of whatever objective ethical facts may exist. This effect is likely to be especially pronounced when it comes to dogmatic religious identities and loyalties, which can be expected to distort ethical perception when it goes against the ethical facts. Suppose, for example, that there are realist ethical facts about gender equality. It should be no surprise that there will nonetheless be disagreement about gender equality if many people's beliefs are distorted by religious commitments inconsistent with it. But again, such disagreement is not epistemically worrisome given this explanation for it.

Finally, we should fully expect ethical insight often to be obscured by personal interests, which can lead to compartmentalized thinking, rationalizations, and other forms of self-deception. This no doubt played a large role in resistance to an ethical acknowledgment of gender and racial equality and their many implications, for example, thus leading to ethical disagreement about all sorts of issues pertaining to gender and race. The same is plausibly true regarding our treatment of nonhuman animals. So given the many interests people may have that are threatened by acknowledgment of certain plausible ethical truths, compounded by the effects of social epistemic environments, it is hardly surprising that there should be widespread ethical disagreement even if there are objective ethical facts. In light of all this, then, the ardent realist will claim that the fact of ethical disagreement does not present a strong case against the existence of objective and knowable ethical truth, inasmuch as such disagreement can plausibly be explained in a way that makes it unsurprising even given the existence of such truth.[40]

(ii) A Positive Account of Ethical Epistemology

On the standard-based model I've proposed for ardent realism, there is no problem gaining knowledge of particular ethical facts *given* background knowledge of the ethical standards: in evaluating an action, for example, one draws on ordinary knowledge of its natural features (the resultance-base properties) and holds it up to the standards in light of these features to see how it fares, that is, what resultant ethical properties it has. This is no more problematic than evaluating chess moves or musical performances and gaining knowledge of their resultant evaluative properties, given knowledge of relevant standards for chess or music. The difficulty lies in explaining how we gain the background

---

[40] This is not to deny that there remain complex and difficult epistemic issues here, especially involving disagreement among well-informed and reflective agents. For detailed discussion of the problem of disagreement, see Enoch (2011, ch. 8).

knowledge of the ethical standards themselves, which is much more complicated than for other kinds of standards.

According to ardent ethical realism, ethical standards cannot be derived from facts about the linguistic and social practices governing our ethical vocabulary, or from the concepts we use, or from scientific facts about biology, psychology, or sociology. In order to meet the relevant desiderata, the ethical standards must instead be grounded in irreducibly evaluative or normative aspects of the world – properties and facts that, like the reason-giving intrinsic badness of suffering and related facts about fitting or unfitting responses to it, are irreducible to empirical ones and not transparent to ordinary empirical inquiry. So in order to apprehend these standards, we must be able to gain knowledge of these irreducibly ethical aspects of things and related facts about them. Perhaps not everyone would have to be able to do this fully since some might rely on testimony in gaining knowledge of ethical standards (though the extent to which one could claim basic ethical knowledge gained through testimony is debatable). But at least some would need to have direct epistemic access to these irreducibly normative aspects of reality. So how do they accomplish that?[41]

This is perhaps the hardest problem for ardent realists, though once again it may not be quite as bad as it initially seems. The problem appears at its worst if we assume that nonnaturalism entails that ethical properties and facts are "causally inert," as logical or mathematical properties and facts are usually taken to be. If the nonnaturalness of ethical properties such as intrinsic badness or inherent worth makes them as causally inert as the property of being a prime number, then we seem to face the same epistemic challenges that plague mathematical Platonism: How would our minds "access" these properties and related facts, which are out there in the world but incapable of affecting us, and so incapable of impinging on our neural states to cause the kinds of changes that would have to accompany changes in our ethical beliefs, for example? And without such access, how can we explain the correlation between our mathematical beliefs and mathematical truths (Field 1989)?

Here again, however, it is important to recall the limited sense in which ardent realism needs to embrace nonnaturalism: it comes to nothing more than the positing of irreducibly normative properties and facts in the world. As we saw earlier, it's not even clear that this should be construed as "nonnaturalist": we

---

[41] David Enoch (2010b) denies that there is any need to explain *epistemic access*, arguing that it is enough if we can explain the substantial correlation between our ethical beliefs and ethical truths. I believe that given an ardent realist framework involving irreducibly normative worldly properties and facts, we do need to explain our ability to epistemically access normative reality in order to account for genuine ethical knowledge. In FitzPatrick (2014c) I explain why I don't think the sort of third-factor explanation Enoch (2010b and 2011, 167 f.) offers to explain the correlation between beliefs and truths is satisfactory.

could just as well expand our conception of the natural to include irreducibly normative properties and facts, just as some physicalists expand the notion of matter or the physical to include irreducibly phenomenal properties and facts. In both cases, we would emphasize that we were never talking about some separate and ethereal realm of strange properties and facts removed from the natural or physical realm, but simply insisting that *the one natural, physical world* in which we live includes aspects that go beyond what is discoverable by scientific inquiry or constructible just from things that are. The ardent realist's task may then be reframed as that of accounting for how we might come to gain knowledge of these irreducibly normative aspects of the *broadly* natural world we already know so much about in other respects.

Once we put it this way, it's unclear why we should assume that just because the items in question are *irreducibly normative* they are "causally inert" in any sense that would "cut us off" epistemically from them. Their lack of transparency to the sciences does imply that they do not have causal powers to affect the natural world *directly*, unmediated by minds, in the way that a magnet has direct causal influence on a piece of iron. The ardent realist certainly needn't claim that the badness of suffering directly causes things to happen in the world, like a magnet. If it could, then it would be scientifically discoverable through such influences, just as magnetism is. But that lack of direct, objective causal influence in the world does not imply that irreducibly normative features of things cannot have any influence on the conscious minds that experience those things.

The intrinsic badness of suffering is not directly going to cause things to happen in the world, but it might plausibly reveal itself to the mind of someone who is experiencing suffering and reflects, using ethical concepts, on its nature. Similarly, with the inherent worth and dignity of people with whom we interact: it cannot be expected to affect scientific instruments, but that does not mean that it cannot reveal itself to us as we engage in ethically significant ways with people and come to appreciate their inherent significance as persons with dignity and worth. In that way, such values could still make a difference to our ethical beliefs, motivations, deliberations, and actions, thus affecting the world *in and through us* as conscious ethical agents.

Of course, it is one thing to open up the possibility of such epistemic access to objective values encountered in the world and quite another to provide a developed positive account of how it all works. How, in interacting empirically with certain worldly things, are we are able also to gain knowledge of their irreducibly normative aspects? How, in interacting with a person in ways that inform us of their rational capacities do we *also* thereby come to appreciate the inherent normative significance they have by virtue of those capacities – their dignity or worth? Obviously, we cannot fairly be expected to provide the sort of empirical causal-mechanistic account naturalists might offer for their moral epistemology. But it would still be nice to have *something* positive to say about how we engage epistemically with these worldly but irreducibly normative properties. And there are at least two challenges here.

One is that it is not clear how much we can expect *philosophy* to be able to tell us about how conscious minds come to be acquainted with such values to yield ethical knowledge. There may simply be limits to what can be said here until we have a much better theoretical understanding of conscious experience itself, perhaps including epistemic roles played by engagement via developed emotional dispositions, since it seems likely that ethically developed emotions will play a part in the story of how we come to understand such things as the dignity or worth of persons and its ramifications. In any case, this is likely an area where ardent ethical realists will have to settle for an account that is more suggestive and less developed than epistemic accounts for reductionist theories.

The second challenge comes from the Darwinian-based worries noted earlier, even if we deny that they "debunk" ethical realism. Ardent ethical realism posits an inherently value-laden world. It also grants that we are products of evolution through Darwinian natural selection, which we have to thank for the basic psychological capacities we draw on in ethical thought and feeling. This doesn't mean that the content of our ethical thought and feeling is pervasively shaped by evolutionary forces, as debunkers often claim (Street 2006). The evolutionary shaping of basic capacities we've inherited is compatible with our developing and shaping those capacities in cultural traditions of intelligent ethical inquiry, and then exercising them in ways that transcend specific evolutionary design, to arrive at largely autonomous content. But it does mean that if we are capable of gaining knowledge of the sort of ethical reality posited by ardent realism, then evolution had to have provided us with basic capacities that could be developed and employed that way. And this may seem quite surprising. Evolution provided these basic psychological capacities for Darwinian reasons having to do with enhancing the reproductive success of our Pleistocene hunter-gatherer ancestors. But the ardent realist does not claim that the irreducibly normative features of things influenced such natural selection processes or even line up very closely with the factors that did.

We seem, therefore, to be stuck with a striking *coincidence*: not only has Darwinian evolution, operating with value-blind biological principles, given rise to entities (sentient and rational beings) that *manifest* inherently value-laden phenomena, but it has made it possible for some of these entities (us) to develop their evolved capacities in such a way as to *grasp* those values. It might seem just a bit too convenient that these two very different spheres of the world should come together like this, with Darwinian processes oriented toward competitive genetic propagation producing entities that both manifest irreducible value and can come to understand and be motivated by it!

This sort of worry is not unique to ardent ethical realism. It parallels a worry that arises for views of consciousness that embrace irreducibly phenomenal properties: somehow, evolutionary processes involving objective physical properties gave rise to entities that manifest irreducibly subjective phenomenal properties as a result of their evolved physical organization. Some of these entities can even develop and exercise their evolved minds to gain rational awareness of aspects of the world transcending anything evolution "designed" them to grasp – such as the very philosophical matters we are presently using our evolved faculties to investigate. As Thomas Nagel (1986) observed, it is striking, to say the least, that the world should happen to work like that.

Some may seek to mitigate such puzzles by adopting a broader metaphysical picture that would help explain these apparent coincidences, such as a theistic framework or a secular one with deeper fundamental laws connecting these different aspects of reality (Nagel 2012). Others may simply be willing to live with such puzzles for the time being, finding that on balance the attractions of these views outweigh this cost. In the case of ardent realism, we may ultimately prefer living with some mystery over accepting the deflation that comes with eliminating it.

References

Alter, Torin and Nagasawa, Yujin, 2015. "What Is Russellian Monism?" in *Consciousness in the Physical World: Perspectives on Russellian Monism*, ed. Alter, T. and Nagasawa, Y., 422–52. Oxford: Oxford University Press.

Berker, Selim, 2019. "Mackie Was Not an Error Theorist," *Philosophical Perspectives* 33: 5–25.

Blackburn, Simon, 1984. *Spreading the Word*. Oxford: Clarendon Press.

1993. *Essays in Quasi-Realism*. Oxford: Oxford University Press.

Boyd, Richard, 1997. "How to Be a Moral Realist," in *Moral Discourse and Practice*, ed. Stephen Darwall, Allan Gibbard, and Peter Railton, 105–36. Oxford: Oxford University Press.

Brink, David, 1989. *Moral Realism and the Foundations of Ethics*. Cambridge: Cambridge University Press.

Conee, Earl, 2016. "A Mysterious Case of Missing Value," *Philosophic Exchange* 45(1): 1–21.

Copp, David, 1995. *Morality, Normativity and Society*. Oxford: Oxford University Press.

2007. *Morality in a Natural World*. Cambridge: Cambridge University Press.

2018. "A Semantic Challenge to Non-Realist Cognitivism," *Canadian Journal of Philosophy* 48: 569–91.

Cuneo, Terence and Shafer-Landau, Russ, 2014. "The Moral Fixed Points: New Directions for Moral Non-Naturalism," *Philosophical Studies* 171(3): 399–443.

Dancy, Jonathan, 1993. *Moral Reasons*. Oxford: Blackwell.

2004. "On the Importance of Making Things Right," *Ratio* 17: 229–37.

2006. "Non-Naturalism," in *The Oxford Handbook of Ethical Theory*, ed. Copp, D., 122–45. Oxford: Oxford University Press.

Dreier, James, 2004. "The Problem of Creeping Minimalism," *Philosophical Perspectives* 18: 23–44.

Eklund, Matti, 2017. *Choosing Normative Concepts*. Oxford: Oxford University Press.

Enoch, David, 2010a. "How Objectivity Matters," in *Oxford Studies in Metaethics, Vol. 5*, ed. Shafer-Landau, R., 111–52. Oxford: Oxford University Press.

2010b. "The Epistemological Challenge to Metanormative Realism: How Best to Understand it and How to Cope with it," *Philosophical Studies* 148(3): 413–38.

2011. *Taking Morality Seriously: A Defense of Robust Realism*. Oxford: Oxford University Press.

Field, Hartry, 1989. *Realism, Mathematics, and Modality*. New York: Basil Blackwell.

FitzPatrick, William, 2000. *Teleology and the Norms of Nature*. New York: Garland.

2004. "Reasons, Value and Particular Agents: Normative Relevance without Motivational Internalism," *Mind* 113(450): 285–318.

2005. "The Practical Turn in Ethical Theory: Korsgaard's Constructivism, Realism, and the Nature of Normativity," *Ethics* 115(4): 651–91.

2008. "Robust Ethical Realism, Non-Naturalism and Normativity," in *Oxford Studies in Metaethics, Vol. 3*, ed. Shafer-Landau, R., 159–205. Oxford: Oxford University Press.

2011. "Ethical Non-Naturalism and Normative Properties," in *New Waves in Metaethics*, ed. Brady, M., 7–35. New York: Palgrave MacMillan.

2013. "How Not to Be an Ethical Constructivist: A Critique of Korsgaard's Neo-Kantian Constitutivism," in *Constructivism in Ethics*, ed. Bagnoli, C., 41–62. Cambridge: Cambridge University Press.

2014a. "Skepticism about Naturalizing Normativity: In Defense of Ethical Non-naturalism," *Res Philosophica* 91(4): 559–88.

2014b. "Debunking Evolutionary Debunking of Ethical Realism," *Philosophical Studies* 172: 883–904.

2014c. "Why There Is No Darwinian Dilemma for Ethical Realism," in *Challenges to Moral and Religious Belief: Disagreement and Evolution*, ed. Bergmann, M. and Kain, P., 237–55. Oxford: Oxford University Press.

2018a. "Ontology for an Uncompromising Ethical Realism," *Topoi* 37(4): 537–47.

2018b. "Representing Ethical Reality," *Canadian Journal of Philosophy* 48 (3–4): 548–68.

2018c. "Open Question Arguments and the Irreducibility of Ethical Normativity," in *The Naturalistic Fallacy*, ed. Sinclair, N., 138–61. Cambridge: Cambridge University Press.

2021. "Moral Phenomenology and the Value-Laden World," *Ethical Theory and Moral Practice*, http://doi.org/10.1007/s10677-021-10213-4.

Forthcoming. "Ardent Moral Realism," in *Oxford Handbook of Moral Realism*, ed. Bloomfield, P. and Copp, D. Oxford: Oxford University Press.

Foot, Philippa, 2001. *Natural Goodness*. Oxford: Oxford University Press.

Gibbard, Allan, 1990. *Wise Choices Apt Feelings*. Cambridge, MA: Harvard University Press.

2003. *Thinking How to Live*. Cambridge, MA: Harvard University Press.

2006. "Normative Properties," in *Metaethics after Moore*, ed. Horgan, T. and Timmons, M., 319–38. Oxford: Oxford University Press.

2010. "How Much Realism? Evolved Thinkers and Normative Concepts," in *Oxford Studies in Metaethics, Vol. 6*, ed. Shafer-Landau, R., 33–51. Oxford: Oxford University Press.

Harman, Gilbert, 1986. "Moral Explanations of Natural Facts – Can Moral Claims Be Tested against Moral Reality?" in Gillespie, N., ed., Spindel Conference: *Moral Realism, The Southern Journal of Philosophy* 24: 57–68.

Horgan, Terry and Timmons, Mark, 1991. "New Wave Moral Realism Meets Moral Twin Earth," *Journal of Philosophical Research* 16: 447–65.

2000. "Non-Descriptivist Cognitivism: Framework for a New Metaethic," *Philosophical Papers* 29: 121–53.

2006. "Expressivism, Yes! Relativism, No!" in *Oxford Studies in Metaethics, Vol. 2*, ed. Shafer-Landau, R., 73–98. Oxford: Oxford University Press.

2008. "What Does Moral Phenomenology Tell Us about Moral Objectivity?" *Social Philosophy & Policy* 25: 267–300.

2018. "The Phenomenology of Moral Authority," in *Moral Skepticism: New Essays*, ed. Machuca, D., 115–40. New York: Routledge.

Huemer, Michael, 2005. *Ethical Intuitionism*. Palgrave Macmillan.

Jackson, Frank, 1998. *From Metaphysics to Ethics*. Oxford: Oxford University Press.

Joyce, Richard, 2002. *The Myth of Morality*. Cambridge: Cambridge University Press.

2003. "Realism and Constructivism in Twentieth Century Moral Philosophy," in *Philosophy in America at the Turn of the Century*, APA Centennial Supplement, *Journal of Philosophical Research*: 99–122.

2006. *The Evolution of Morality*. Cambridge, MA: MIT Press.

Kitcher, Philip, 2006. "Biology and Ethics," in David Copp, ed., The Oxford Handbook of Ethical Theory, Oxford: Oxford University Press, 163–85.

2011. The Ethical Project. Cambridge, MA: Harvard University Press.

Korsgaard, Christine, 1996. *The Sources of Normativity*. Cambridge: Cambridge University Press.

2009. *Self-Constitution*. Oxford: Oxford University Press.

Leary, Stephanie, 2017. "Non-Naturalism and Normative Necessities," in *Oxford Studies in Metaethics, Vol. 12*, ed. Shafer-Landau, R., 76–105. Oxford: Oxford University Press.

Mackie, John. L., 1977. *Ethics: Inventing Right and Wrong*. Harmondsworth: Penguin.

McPherson, Tristram, 2012. "Ethical Non-Naturalism and the Metaphysics of Supervenience," in *Oxford Studies in Metaethics, Vol. 7*, ed. Shafer-Landau, R., 205–34. Oxford: Oxford University Press.

Mintz-Woo, Kian, 2018. "On Parfit's Ontology," *Canadian Journal of Philosophy* 48(5): 707–25.

Moore, G. E., 1903. *Principia Ethica*, edited and with an introduction by Thomas Baldwin, rev. ed. Cambridge: Cambridge University Press, 1994.

Moosavi, Parisa, 2019. "From Biological Functions to Natural Goodness," *Philosopher's Imprint* 19(51): 1–20.

Nagel, Thomas, 1986. *The View from Nowhere*. Oxford: Oxford University Press.
  2012. *Mind and Cosmos*. Oxford: Oxford University Press.

Parfit, Derek, 2011. *On What Matters, Vol. 2*. Oxford: Oxford University Press.
  2017. *On What Matters*, Vol. 3. Oxford: Oxford University Press.

Russell, Bertrand, 1927. *The Analysis of Matter*. London: Kegan Paul.

Sayre-McCord, Geoffrey, 1988. "The Many Moral Realisms," in *Essays on Moral Realism*, ed. Sayre-McCord, G., 1–26. Ithaca: Cornell University Press.

Scanlon, Thomas, 2014. *Being Realistic about Reasons*. Oxford: Oxford University Press.

Schroeder, Mark, 2005. "Realism and Reduction: The Quest for Robustness," *Philosopher's Imprint* 5(1): 1–17.

Shafer-Landau, Russ, 2003. *Moral Realism: A Defence*. Oxford: Oxford University Press.
  2012. "Evolutionary Debunking, Moral Realism and Moral Knowledge," *Journal of Ethics and Social Philosophy* 7(1): 1–37.

Smith, Michael, 2004. *Ethics and the A Priori*. Cambridge: Cambridge University Press.

Strawson, Galen, 2015. "Real Materialism (with New Postscript)," in *Consciousness in the Physical World: Perspectives on Russellian Monism*, ed. Alter, T. and Nagasawa, Y., 161–208. Oxford: Oxford University Press.

Street, Sharon, 2006. "A Darwinian Dilemma for Realist Theories of Value," *Philosophical Studies* 127: 109–66.
  2008a. "Reply to Copp: Naturalism, Normativity, and the Varieties of Realism Worth Worrying about," *Philosophical Issues* 18: 207–28.
  2008b. "Constructivism about Reasons," in *Oxford Studies in Metaethics, Vol. 3*, ed. Shafer-Landau, R., 207–46. Oxford: Oxford University Press.

Sturgeon, Nicholas, 1986. "Harman on Moral Explanations of Natural Facts," in Gillespie, N., ed., Spindel Conference: *Moral Realism, The Southern Journal of Philosophy* 24: 69–78.

1988. "Moral Explanations," in *Essays on Moral Realism*, ed. Sayre-McCord, G., 229–55. Ithaca: Cornell University Press.

2003. "Moore on Ethical Naturalism," *Ethics* 113(3): 528–56.

2006. "Ethical Naturalism," in *The Oxford Handbook of Ethical Theory*, ed. Copp, D., 91–121. Oxford: Oxford University Press.

Suikkanen, Jussi, 2017. "Non-Realist Cognitivism, Truth, and Objectivity," *Acta Analytica* 32: 193–212.

Williams, Bernard, 1981. "Internal and External Reasons," in his *Moral Luck*, 101–13. Cambridge: Cambridge University Press.

Wright, Larry, 1976. *Teleological Explanations*. Berkeley: University of California Press.

Acknowledgments

I am grateful to Robert Audi, David Copp, Ben Eggleston, Dale Miller, and Russ Shafer-Landau for helpful comments on a draft of this Element.

Cambridge Elements ≡

Ethics

Ben Eggleston
University of Kansas

Ben Eggleston is a professor of philosophy at the University of Kansas. He is the editor of John Stuart Mill, *Utilitarianism: With Related Remarks from Mill's Other Writings* (Hackett, 2017) and a coeditor of *Moral Theory and Climate Change: Ethical Perspectives on a Warming Planet* (Routledge, 2020), *The Cambridge Companion to Utilitarianism* (Cambridge, 2014), and *John Stuart Mill and the Art of Life* (Oxford, 2011). He is also the author of numerous articles and book chapters on various topics in ethics.

Dale E. Miller
Old Dominion University, Virginia

Dale E. Miller is a professor of philosophy at Old Dominion University. He is the author of *John Stuart Mill: Moral, Social and Political Thought* (Polity, 2010) and a coeditor of *Moral Theory and Climate Change: Ethical Perspectives on a Warming Planet* (Routledge, 2020), *A Companion to Mill* (Blackwell, 2017), *The Cambridge Companion to Utilitarianism* (Cambridge, 2014), *John Stuart Mill and the Art of Life* (Oxford, 2011), and *Morality, Rules, and Consequences: A Critical Reader* (Edinburgh, 2000). He is also the editor-in-chief of *Utilitas*, and the author of numerous articles and book chapters on various topics in ethics broadly construed.

About the Series

This Elements series provides an extensive overview of major figures, theories, and concepts in the field of ethics. Each entry in the series acquaints students with the main aspects of its topic while articulating the author's distinctive viewpoint in a manner that will interest researchers.

Cambridge Elements ≡

Ethics

Printed in the United States
by Baker & Taylor Publisher Services